CW01455570

This document is geared towards providing exact reliable information with regard to the topic and issue covered.

The publication is sold with the idea that the publisher is not required to render accounting, officially permitted, or otherwise, qualified services. If advice is necessary, legal or professional, a practiced individual in the profession should be ordered.From a Declaration of Principles which was accepted and approved equally by a Committee of the American Bar Association and a Commit tee of Publishers and Associations.

The information provided herein is stated to be truthful and consistent, in that any liability, in terms of inattention or otherwise, by any usage or abuse of any po

licies, processes, or directions contained within is the solitary and utter responsibility of the recipient

1

Table of Contents

Chapter 1 Polyvagal Theory

BRIEF HISTORY ON THE AUTONOMIC NERVOUS SYSTEM

The visceral organs as regulated by the central nervous system has reshaped the scope of physiological studies by being the focal point in various historical publications. The dynamic link (neural) between a man's mind and heart was first proposed in 1872 by a great scientist. At the point when the heart is influenced it responds on the mind; furthermore, the condition of the mind again responds through the pneumo-gastric [vagus] nerve on the heart; so that under any fervor there will be a lot of common activity and response between these, the two most significant organs of the body. Even though the scientist recognized the bi-directional correspondence between the viscera and the cerebrum, a consequent formal depiction of the autonomic nervous system limited the significance of focal administrative structures and afferents. Furthermore, research carried out in the medical and physiological field would bring to light, in general, the peripheral engine nerves of the autonomic nervous system, with a theoretical accentuation on the combined hostility between sympathetic and parasympathetic efferent pathways on the objective visceral organs. This center limited intrigue in both afferent pathways and the brainstem regions that control specific efferent pathways. The early conceptualization of the vagus centered on an undifferentiated efferent pathway that was accepted to tweak "tone" simultaneously to a few target organs. In this manner, brainstem territories directing the supradiaphragmatic (eg, myelinated vagal pathways beginning in the core ambiguous and ending basically over the stomach) were not practically recognized from those controlling the subdiaphragmatic (eg, unmyelinated vagal pathways starting in the dorsal engine core of the vagus and ending essentially underneath the stomach). Without this qualification, research and hypothesis concentrated on the matched opposition between the parasympathetic and sympathetic innervation to target organs. The outcome of accentuation on matched enmity was an acknowledgment in physiology and prescription of worldwide builds, for example, autonomic equalization, sympathetic tone, and vagal tone.

Over 50 years back, it was recommended that the autonomic sensory system was not exclusively vegetative and programmed however was rather an incorporated framework with both fringe and focal neurons. By underscoring the focal components that intercede the dynamic guideline of fringe organs, it was foreseen that the requirement for advancements to constantly screen fringe and focal neural circuits associated with the guideline of instinctive capacity.

Autonomic Nervous System

The autonomic nervous system (ANS), once in the past the vegetative sensory system, is a division of the fringe sensory system that provisions smooth muscle and organs, and along these lines impacts the capacity of interior organs. The autonomic nervous system is a control framework that demonstrates to a great extent unknowingly and directs in essence capacities, for example, the pulse, processing, respiratory rate, pupillary reaction, pee, and sexual arousal. This framework is the essential instrument in charge of the reaction fight-or-flight.

In mind, the autonomic nervous system is directed by the nerve center. The control of breath, the heart guideline (the cardiovascular control focus), the vasomotor action (the vasomotor focus), and certain reflex activities are all incorporated the autonomic capacity, for example, hacking, sniffling, gulping and spewing. Those are then subdivided into different territories and are likewise connected to ANS subsystems and sensory systems outer to the cerebrum. The nerve center, simply over the mind stem, goes about as an integrator for autonomic capacities, getting ANS administrative contribution from the limbic framework to do so.

The autonomic sensory system has three branches: the sympathetic sensory system, the parasympathetic sensory system, and the enteric apprehensive system. Some course readings do exclude the enteric sensory system as a major aspect of this system. The sympathetic sensory system is frequently considered the "fight or flight" framework, while the parasympathetic sensory system is regularly considered the "rest and summary" or "feed and breed" framework. Much of the time, both of these frameworks have "inverse" activities where one framework actuates a physiological reaction and the different restrains it. A more established rearrangement of the sympathetic and parasympathetic sensory systems as "excitatory" and "inhibitory" was toppled because of the numerous exemptions found. A progressively current portrayal is that the sympathetic sensory system is a "brisk reaction assembling framework" and the parasympathetic is an "all the more gradually initiated hosing framework", yet even this has special cases, for example, in sexual excitement and climax, wherein both play a role.

There are inhibitory and excitatory neurotransmitters between neurons. Generally, as of late, a third subsystem of neurons that have been named non-noradrenergic, non-cholinergic transmitters (since they utilize nitric oxide as a synapse) have been portrayed and seen as fundamental in autonomic capacity, specifically in the gut and the lungs.

Even though the ANS is otherwise called the instinctive sensory system, the ANS is just associated with the engine side. Most self-governing capacities are automatic however they can regularly work related to the physical sensory system which gives intentional control.

The autonomic sensory system, demonstrating splanchnic nerves in the center, and the vagus nerve as "X" in blue. The heart and organs underneath in rundown to the right are viewed as viscera.

The autonomic sensory system is separated into the sympathetic sensory system and parasympathetic sensory system. The sympathetic division rises out of the spinal rope in the thoracic and lumbar regions. The parasympathetic division has craniosacral "outpouring", implying that the neurons start at the cranial nerves (explicitly the oculomotor nerve, facial nerve, glossopharyngeal nerve, and vagus nerve) and sacral (S2-S4) spinal line.

The autonomic sensory system is one of a kind in that it requires a successive two-neuron efferent pathway; the preganglionic neuron should the first neurotransmitter onto a postganglionic neuron before innervating the objective organ. The preganglionic, or first, the neuron will start at the "surge" and will neurotransmitter at the postganglionic, or second, neuron's cell body. The postganglionic neuron will then neurotransmitter at the objective organ.

Sympathetic division: Sympathetic sensory system

The sympathetic sensory system comprises of cells with bodies in the sidelong dark section from T1 to L2/3. These cell bodies are "GVE" (general instinctive efferent) neurons and are the preganglionic neurons. There are a few areas whereupon preganglionic neurons can neurotransmitter for their postganglionic neurons:

Paravertebral ganglia of the sympathetic chain (This sudden spike in demand for either side of the vertebral bodies), cervical ganglia, Thoracic ganglia and rostral lumbar ganglia, Caudal lumbar ganglia and sacral ganglia, Prevertebral ganglia (celiac ganglion, aorticorenal ganglion, predominant mesenteric ganglion, substandard mesenteric ganglion)

Chromaffin cells of the adrenal medulla (this is the one special case to the two-neuron pathway rule: the neurotransmitter is legitimately efferent onto the objective cell bodies). These ganglia give the postganglionic neurons from which innervation of target organs follows. Instances of splanchnic (instinctive) nerves are: Cervical heart nerves and thoracic instinctive nerves, which neural connection in the sympathetic chain

Thoracic splanchnic nerves (more prominent, lesser, least), which neural connection in the prevertebral ganglia. Lumbar splanchnic nerves, which neurotransmitter in the prevertebral ganglia, Sacral splanchnic nerves, which neurotransmitter in the substandard hypogastric plexus. These all contain afferent (tactile) nerves too, known as general instinctive afferent neurons.

Parasympathetic sensory system:

The parasympathetic sensory system comprises of cells situated in one of two areas: the brainstem (Cranial Nerves III, VII, IX, X) or the sacral spinal line (S2, S3, S4). These are the preganglionic neurons, which neurotransmitter with postganglionic neurons in these areas:

• Parasympathetic ganglia of the head: Ciliary (Cranial nerve III), Submandibular (Cranial nerve VII), Pterygopalatine (Cranial nerve VII), and Otic (Cranial nerve IX)

• In or close to the mass of an organ innervated by the Vagus (Cranial nerve X) or Sacral nerves (S2, S3, S4)

These ganglia give the postganglionic neurons from which innervations of target organs follows. Models are:

• The postganglionic parasympathetic splanchnic (instinctive) nerves

• The Vagus nerve, which goes through the thorax and stomach locales innervating, among different organs, the heart, lungs, liver and stomach

Tangible neurons: Sensory neuron

The tangible arm is made out of essential instinctive tactile neurons found in the fringe sensory system (PNS), in cranial tangible ganglia: the geniculate, petrosal and nodose ganglia, annexed separately to cranial nerves VII, IX, and X. These tactile neurons screen the degrees of carbon dioxide, oxygen and sugar in the blood, blood vessel pressure and the substance structure of the stomach and gut content. They additionally pass on the feeling of taste and smell, which, in contrast to most elements of the ANS, is a cognizant recognition. Blood oxygen and carbon dioxide are in reality legitimately detected by the carotid body, a little assortment of chemosensors at the bifurcation of the carotid supply route, innervated by the petrosal (9th) ganglion. Essential tactile neurons venture (neurotransmitter) onto "second request" instinctive tangible neurons situated in the medulla oblongata, shaping the core of the singular tract (nTS), that coordinates all instinctive data. The nTS additionally gets contribution from a close-by chemosensory focus, the territory postrema, that identifies poisons in the blood and the cerebrospinal liquid and is fundamental for artificially prompted spewing or contingent taste revulsion (the memory that guarantees that a creature that has been harmed by nourishment never contacts it again). This instinctive tangible data continually and unwittingly balances the movement of the engine neurons of the ANS.

Stimulation

Autonomic nerves travel to organs all through the body. Most organs get parasympathetic stockpile by the vagus nerve and sympathetic inventory by splanchnic nerves. The tactile piece of the last arrives at the spinal segment at certain spinal fragments. Agony in any interior organ is seen as alluded torment, all the more explicitly as torment from the dermatome relating to the spinal segment.

Motor neuron (Engine neurons)

Engine neurons of the autonomic sensory system are found in "autonomic ganglia". Those of the parasympathetic branch is found near the objective organ while the ganglia of the sympathetic branch are found near the spinal string.

The sympathetic ganglia here, are found in two chains: the pre-vertebral and pre-aortic chains. The movement of autonomic ganglionic neurons is balanced by "preganglionic neurons" situated in the focal sensory system. Preganglionic sympathetic neurons are situated in the spinal string, at the thorax and upper lumbar levels. Preganglionic parasympathetic neurons are found in the medulla oblongata where they structure instinctive engine cores; the dorsal engine core of the vagus nerve; the core ambiguous, the salivatory cores, and in the sacral district of the spinal rope.

Function: Capacity of the autonomic sensory system

Sympathetic and parasympathetic divisions commonly work contrary to one another. In any case, this restriction is better-named correlative in nature as opposed to adversarial. For a similarity, one may think about the sympathetic division as the quickening agent and the parasympathetic division as the brake. The sympathetic division ordinarily works in activities requiring brisk reactions. The parasympathetic division capacities with activities that don't require a quick response. The sympathetic framework is frequently considered the "fight or flight" framework, while the parasympathetic framework is regularly considered the "rest and review" or "feed and breed" framework.

Be that as it may, numerous cases of sympathetic and parasympathetic movement can't be credited to "fight" or "rest" circumstances. For instance, standing up from a leaning back or sitting position would involve an impractical drop in circulatory strain notwithstanding a compensatory increment in the blood vessel sympathetic tonus. Another model is the steady, second-to-second, tweak of the pulse by sympathetic and parasympathetic impacts, as an element of the respiratory cycles. As a rule, these two frameworks ought to be viewed as forever regulating crucial capacities, in generally adversarial design, to accomplish homeostasis. Higher living beings keep up their honesty utilizing homeostasis which depends on negative criticism guideline which, thusly, commonly relies upon the autonomic apprehensive system. Some commonplace activities of the sympathetic and parasympathetic sensory systems are recorded below.

Sympathetic anxious system: Sympathetic sensory system

Advances a fight-or-flight reaction, compares with excitement and vitality age and represses processing

• Diverts bloodstream away from the gastrointestinal (GI) tract and skin through vasoconstriction

• Bloodstream to skeletal muscles and the lungs is upgraded (by as much as 1200% on account of skeletal muscles)

• Dilates bronchioles of the lung through circling epinephrine, which takes into consideration more noteworthy alveolar oxygen trade

• Increases pulse and the contractility of cardiovascular cells (myocytes), along these lines giving a system to the improved blood stream to skeletal muscles

• Dilates understudies and loosens up the ciliary muscle to the focal point, enabling more light to enter the eye and improves far vision

• Provides vasodilation for the coronary vessels of the heart

• Constricts all the intestinal sphincters and the urinary sphincter

• Inhibits peristalsis

• Stimulates climax

Parasympathetic sensory system

The parasympathetic sensory system has been said to advance a "rest and review" reaction, advances quieting of the nerves come back to normal capacity, and improving assimilation. Elements of nerves inside the parasympathetic sensory system include:

• Dilating veins prompting the GI tract, expanding the bloodstream.

• Constricting the bronchiolar breadth when the requirement for oxygen has lessened

• Dedicated cardiovascular parts of the vagus and thoracic spinal adornment nerves bestow parasympathetic control of the heart (myocardium)

• Constriction of the understudy and constriction of the ciliary muscles, encouraging settlement and taking into account nearer vision

• Stimulating salivary organ emission, and quickens peristalsis, intervening processing of nourishment and, in a roundabout way, the assimilation of supplements

• Sexual. Nerves of the fringe sensory system are engaged with the erection of genital tissues utilizing the pelvic splanchnic nerves 2–4. They are likewise answerable for invigorating sexual excitement.

Enteric sensory system

The enteric sensory system is the inborn sensory system of the gastrointestinal framework. It has been depicted as "the Second Brain of the Human Body". Its capacities include:

• Sensing compound and mechanical changes in the gut

• Regulating emissions in the gut

• Controlling peristalsis and some different developments

Neurotransmitters

A stream graph indicating the procedure of incitement of adrenal medulla that makes it discharge adrenaline, that further follows up on adrenoreceptors, in a roundabout way interceding or mirroring sympathetic movement.

At the effector organs, sympathetic ganglionic neurons discharge noradrenaline (norepinephrine), alongside different co-transmitters, for example, ATP, to follow up on adrenergic receptors, except for the perspiration organs and the adrenal medulla:

• Acetylcholine is the preganglionic synapse for the two divisions of the ANS, just as the postganglionic synapse of parasympathetic neurons. Nerves that discharge acetylcholine is said to be cholinergic. In the parasympathetic framework, ganglionic neurons use acetylcholine as a synapse to invigorate muscarinic receptors.

• At the adrenal medulla, there is no postsynaptic neuron. Rather the presynaptic neuron discharges acetylcholine to follow up on nicotinic receptors. Incitement of the adrenal medulla discharges adrenaline (epinephrine) into the circulation system, which follows up on adrenoceptors, in this way in a roundabout way interceding or impersonating sympathetic action.

Caffeine effects

Caffeine is a bioactive fixing found in generally devoured drinks, for example, espresso, tea, and soft drinks. Transient physiological impacts of caffeine incorporate expanded pulse and nerve outpouring. Constant utilization of caffeine may hinder physiological momentary impacts. Utilization of jazzed coffee expands parasympathetic action in constant caffeine purchasers; in any case, decaffeinated coffee restrains parasympathetic movement in ongoing caffeine buyers. It is conceivable that other bioactive fixings in decaffeinated coffee may likewise add to the restraint of parasympathetic movement in constant caffeine consumers.

Caffeine is fit for expanding the work limit while people perform strenuous errands. In one investigation, caffeine incited a more prominent most extreme pulse while a strenuous errand was being performed contrasted with a fake treatment. This inclination is likely because of caffeine's capacity to increment sympathetic nerve outpouring. Besides, this investigation found that recuperation after extraordinary exercise was more slow when caffeine was devoured before work out. This discovering is demonstrative of caffeine's propensity to hinder parasympathetic action in non-routine purchasers. The caffeine-animated increment in nerve movement is probably going to bring out other physiological impacts as the body endeavors to keep up homeostasis.

The impacts of caffeine on parasympathetic action may differ contingent upon the situation of the person when autonomic reactions are estimated. One examination found that the situated position restrained autonomic movement after caffeine utilization (75 mg); nonetheless, parasympathetic action expanded in the recumbent position. This finding may clarify why some ongoing caffeine purchasers (75 mg or less) don't encounter momentary impacts of caffeine if their routine requires numerous hours in a situated position. Note that the information supporting expanded parasympathetic action in the recumbent position was gotten from an examination including members between the ages of 25 and 30 who were viewed as sound and inactive. Caffeine may impact autonomic action contrastingly for people who are progressively dynamic or elderly.

What Is the Polyvagal Theory?

The phylogeny of the visceral nervous system of vertebrates, exposed the vagal paradox when critically analyzed. This exposure engineered various researches in both neuroanatomy and neurophysiology, these researches carried out over the years have helped in the streamlining of the vagus nerve into two main parts, these parts cover the versatile and complex social behavior and adaptive capabilities of a mammal. The effect of this theory as propounded is seen in the irregular rhythmic heartbeats, the variance in the heart rhythm of over a 100 beat per second and rhythm of lower than 60 beats per second. Even though the slower rhythms have been accepted to have a sympathetic influence, they are hindered by atropine.

The polyvagal theory, however, expresses how these three phylogenetic phases in the improvement of the vertebrate visceral nervous system are related to a unique involuntary subsystem that is revealed in higher animals(mammals). These autonomic subsystems are phylogenetically requested and typically connected to communicating socially like appearance, vocals and tuning in, to preparation as in fight-flight practices, and to immobilization like in pretending to be dead, vasovagal syncope, and shutting down behaviorally. The social correspondence framework i.e social commitment framework, which includes the myelinated vagus, serves as a calmer by sending a sympathetic impulse to the heart and decreasing the hypothalamus, pituitary, and adrenal gland axis. The sympathetic part of the autonomic nervous system controls the mobilization systems. The most phylogenetically crude part, the immobilization framework, is reliant on the unmyelinated vagus, which is imparted to most vertebrates. With expanded neural intricacy coming about because of phylogenetic advancement, the creature's social and emotional collection is enhanced. The three circuits can be conceptualized as dynamic, giving versatile reactions to sheltered, perilous, and dangerous occasions and settings.

Polyvagal Theory indicates two unmistakable parts of the vagus, or tenth cranial nerve. These incorporate a phylogenetically more seasoned branch starting in the dorsal engine core (DMX), furthermore, a more up to date branch starting in the core ambiguous (NA). The DMX and NA are situated in the dorsal and ventral vagal edifices, separately, contiguous neural structures in the medulla. Albeit the two branches give an inhibitory contribution to the heart employing the parasympathetic sensory system (PNS),1 they do as such in the administration of unmistakable transformative capacities. The DMX branch once in a while alluded to as the vegetative vagus is established in the essential endurance procedure of crude vertebrates, creatures of land and water, and reptiles, which freeze when undermined. In like manner, the vegetative vagus capacities to smother metabolic requests under states of peril. Interestingly, the NA branch, or shrewd vagus, is unmistakably mammalian, and advanced vagus is related to the desire to powerfully control significantly expanded metabolic yield. This incorporates regulation of fight/flight (F/F) reacting in the administration of social affiliative practices. In the wake of situating to conspecific, warm-blooded creatures should either take part in social association or start F/F reacting. The previous requires continued consideration, which is joined by vagally intervened pulse deceleration. Conversely, battling and escaping are portrayed by anger and frenzy, separately, which are related to close to finish a vagal withdrawal. This encourages enormous increments in heart yield by the sympathetic sensory system (SSS), which is never again restricted by inhibitory vagal impacts. In this manner, the brilliant vagus restrains acceleratory SNS contribution to the heart when continued consideration and additionally social commitment are versatile, and pulls back this inhibitory impact when battling or escaping are versatile. Even though the above portrayal has clear ramifications for psychopathology, two extra traits of Polyvagal Theory must be taken into consideration before continuing. To begin with, the practical association of the mammalian autonomic sensory system (ANS) is assumed to be phylogenetically arranged in various levels, with both vagal branches additionally innervate other objective organs that are not the core interest of this paper. Intrigued perusers are alluded response techniques to risk directed by the most up to date neural structures at first, trailed by the following most up to date structures when a given reaction system falls flat. Along these lines, if vagally intervened social affiliative practices are inadequate in adapting to a boost, reaction systems move to F/F practices, intervened by the phylogenetically more seasoned SNS. If F/F reacting likewise falls flat, immobilization practices are started, which are interceded by the vegetative vagus, the most seasoned accessible reaction framework. Second, feeling guidelines and social connections are viewed as developing characteristics of the administrative capacities served by the savvy vagus. Arrangement of the more current vagal framework smothers the hearty passionate responses that describe F/F reacting, an essential for the rise of complex social conduct. Progressive association of the ANS, combined with the adjusting impacts of the shrewd vagus on SNS-intervened F/F reacting, proposes that practical lacks of the keen vagus should put people in danger for passionate lability, a sign of psychopathology. Besides, since F/F reaction inclinations bring out solid methodology (outrage) furthermore, evasion (wretchedness, tension) feelings, diminished heart vagal tone should be seen over a wide scope of mental conditions in which dysregulated feeling happens. Steady with this expectation, the constricted vagal tone has been watched among withdrawn and parasuicidal kids and young people, quality antagonistic grown-ups, and discouraged, on edge, and frenzy disarranged gatherings. Besides, over the top vagal reactivity to different difficulties has been seen among youngsters who are both inconsistently bashful and indignantly receptive, and with extreme cases patients. Conversely, vagal tone is emphatically connected with youngsters' social commitment, with educator reports of social ability, and with articulations of sympathy toward others in trouble. These discoveries are steady with the theory that the ventral vagal complex advanced to encourage social correspondence and feel guidelines. High vagal tone additionally seems to cradle youngsters who witness conjugal clash and antagonistic vibe from the related danger of creating both disguising and externalizing conduct designs.

As the above dialog proposes it is presently settled that insufficient vagal tone and exorbitant vagal reactivity mark an expansive scope of mental issue and the seemingly normal condition among these is dysregulated feeling. It is likewise settled that cardiovascular vagal tone marks person contrasts in feeling guideline abilities. Polyvagal Theory gives a setting to understanding feeling dysregulation as a disappointment of the phylogenetically more up to date vagal framework, which results in the organization of SNS-intervened F/F reaction procedures in circumstances where they are not versatile. However, on the off chance that we acknowledge the premise that interruptions in vagal working potentiate F/F reacting, and this adds to the improvement and support of psychopathology, we are still left with the question of why some genuinely labile people react all the more regularly with appetitive (counting fight) practices, as in the instance of externalizing issue, while others react all the more regularly with aversive (counting flight) practices, as on account of disguising scatters. Steady with Polyvagal Theory, we have contended that both fight and flight practices are intervened incidentally by the SNS and that speculations of appetitive and aversive inspiration must be considered to represent the dominating reaction set (approach versus evasion) seen in various types of psychopathology. In particular, we have contended that an under-responsive focal prize framework, bringing about a constantly touchy temperament state, combined with inadequate vagal regulation of feeling, prompts the sensation looking for and forceful practices normal for direct confusion and wrongdoing. Conversely, an over-responsive focal restraint framework, bringing about high attribute tension, combined with the inadequate vagal tweak of feeling, prompts the withdrawal practices normal for nervousness and frenzy scatters. This detailing depends intensely on Gray's hypothesis of inspiration. Given broad creature and pharmacological work, Gray proposed a conduct approach framework (BAS) and a conduct hindrance framework (BIS). The BAS oversees appetitive practices in light of remuneration and is interceded by dopaminergic pathways including the ventral tegmental territory and the core accumbens of the ventral striatum. These neural structures are injected with dopamine following appetitive practices, bringing about post-consummatory pleasurable full of feeling states. Later neuroimaging contemplates have uncovered under-action in the striatum and its frontal projections among externalizing youngsters and teenagers, which gives off an impression of being incompletely standardized by methylphenidate organization. Thusly, low focal dopamine movement has been related to attribute peevishness which may lead influenced people to look for bigger and bigger prizes to accomplish fortifying degrees of post-consummatory satisfaction. It merits reemphasizing that steady with Polyvagal Theory, we have stated that BAS dysregulation is especially tricky when combined with lacking the vagal balance of negative feeling, and that proficient feeling guideline serves to cushion youngsters who are in danger for sensation looking for and hostility because of constantly low focal dopamine action.

As opposed to the BAS, the BIS restrains prepotent practices at the point when struggle emerges due to contending persuasive goals.These contending targets may speak to approach–approach clashes, shirking evasion clashes, or approach–evasion clashes. BIS initiation incites nervousness, which encourages practices planned for settling the dissimilar inspirational objectives. The BIS is interceded by a system of neural structures including the amygdala and the septohippocampal framework. Although the BIS won't be examined further in this paper because of space requirements, exorbitant BIS movement has been connected to elevated hazard for disguising disarranges, though insufficient BIS movement has been connected to social disinhibition.

In the segments to pursue, we talk about three investigations of externalizing conduct traversing preschool to puberty and depict how polyvagal, persuasive, and social fortification hypotheses.

Why The Discovery Of Polyvagal Theory Matters?

Envisioning the structure of a brain can be compared to imagining a sea tempest. Although we can envision a terrible climate, it is more difficult to envision changing that climate. In any case, the polyvagal hypothesis gives psychological instructors a valuable image of the sensory system that aides them in helping clients better.

the polyvagal hypothesis was postulated out of rigorous research on the vagus nerve. The vagus nerve serves the parasympathetic sensory system, which is the quieting part of our sensory system mechanics. The parasympathetic piece of the autonomic sensory system adjusts the sympathetic dynamic part, however is substantially more nuanced ways than we comprehended before the polyvagal hypothesis.

Before the polyvagal hypothesis, our sensory system was envisioned as a two-section hostile framework, with more triggers showing signs of less relief and vis-a-vis. Polyvagal hypothesis recognizes a third kind of sensory system reaction that was discovered was called the social commitment framework, a fun-loving blend of actuation and quieting that works out of interesting nerve impact.

The social commitment framework causes medical practitioners to explore connections. Helping patients move into the utilization of their social commitment framework, which enables them to turn out to be progressively adaptable in their adapting styles.

The two different pieces of our sensory system capacity to assist us with overseeing perilous circumstances. Most advocates are now acquainted with the two resistance instruments activated by these two pieces of the sensory system: sympathetic fight-or-flight and parasympathetic shutdown, at times called freeze-or-black out. Utilization of our social commitment framework, then again, requires a feeling of wellbeing.

Polyvagal hypothesis encourages us to comprehend that the two parts of the vagus nerve quiet the body, yet they do so in various ways. Shutdown, or freeze-or-black out, happens through the dorsal part of the vagus nerve. This response can feel like the exhausted muscles and discombobulation of awful influenza. At the point when the dorsal vagal nerve closes down the body, it can move us into fixed status or separation. Notwithstanding influencing the heart and lungs, the dorsal branch influences the body working underneath the stomach and is associated with stomach related problems.

The central part of the vagal nerve influences the body working over the stomach. This is the branch that serves the social commitment framework. The ventral vagal nerve hoses the body's routinely dynamic state. Picture controlling a steed as you ride it back to the stable. You would keep on pulling back on and discharge the reins in nuanced approaches to guarantee that the pony keeps up a fitting pace. Similarly, the ventral vagal nerve permits initiation in a nuanced way, along these lines offering an unexpected quality in comparison to sympathetic enactment.

Ventral vagal discharge into action takes milliseconds, while sympathetic enactment takes seconds and includes different concoction responses that are much the same as losing the pony's reins. What's more, when the fight-or-flight concoction responses have started, it can take our bodies 10–20 minutes to come back to our pre-fight/pre-flight state. Ventral vagal discharge into action doesn't include these sorts of synthetic responses. Subsequently, we can make speedier modifications among actuation and quieting, like what we can do when we utilize the reins to control the pony.

On the off chance that you go to a canine park, you will see certain mutts that are apprehensive. They show fight or-flight practices. Different pooches will flag a desire to play. This flagging regularly takes the structure that we people commandeered for the descending confronting hound present in yoga. At the point when a pooch gives this sign, it prompts a degree of excitement that can be exceptional. Notwithstanding, this fun-loving vitality has an altogether different soul than the force of fight-or-flight practices. This perky soul describes the social commitment framework. At the point when we experience our condition as protected, we work from our social commitment framework.

If we have an uncertain injury from before, we may live in the form of interminable fight-or-flight. We might have the option to channel this fight-or-flight tension into exercises, for example, cleaning the house, raking the forgets about or working at the rec center, yet these exercises will have an unexpected vibe in comparison to they would if they were finished with social commitment science (think "Whistle While You Work").

For some injury survivors, no action effectively channels their fight-or-flight sensations. Accordingly, they feel caught and their bodies shut down. These customers may live in the form of the never-ending shutdown.

An outstanding scientist, who happens to be a long-lasting companion and associate of the Polyvagal theory creator, has considered the shutdown reaction through creature perceptions and bodywork with customers. In Waking the Tiger: Healing Trauma, he clarifies that rising out of shutdown requires a shiver or shake to release suspended fight or-flight vitality. In a hazardous circumstance, if we have shut down and an open door for dynamic endurance presents itself, we can wake ourselves up. As advisors, we may perceive this move from shutdown to fight or-trip in a customer's move from melancholy into nervousness.

Be that as it may, how might we help our customers move into their social commitment science? On the off chance that customers live in a progressively dissociative, discouraged, shutdown way, we should assist them with moving incidentally into fight-or-flight. As customers experience fight-or-flight power, we should then assist them in finding a feeling of security. At the point when they can detect that they are protected, they can move into their social commitment framework.

The body-mindfulness procedures that are a piece of intellectual conduct treatment (CBT) and rationalistic conduct treatment (DBT) can assist customers with moving out of dissociative, shutdown reactions by urging them to turn out to be increasingly exemplified. At the point when customers are increasingly present in their bodies and better ready to take care of fleeting solid pressure, they can wake up from a shutdown reaction. As customers actuate out of shutdown and move toward fight-

or-flight sensations, the idea rebuilding procedures that are likewise part of CBT and DBT can instruct customers to assess their security all the more precisely. Intelligent listening procedures can assist customers with feeling an association with their instructors. This makes it feasible for these customers to have a sense of security enough to move into social commitment science.

Explicit Parts of Ventral Vagal Nerve Working

Polyvagal theory creator picked the name social commitment framework because the ventral vagal nerve influences the center ear, which sift through foundation clamors to make it simpler to hear the human voice. It additionally influences facial muscles and along these lines the capacity to make informative outward appearances. At long last, it influences the larynx and in this manner vocal tone and vocal designing, helping people make sounds that relieve each other.

train center ear muscles. Customers with poor social commitment framework working may have inward ear challenges that make it difficult for them to get alleviating from others' voices. As guides, we can be aware of our vocal examples and outward appearances and inquisitive about the impacts those parts of our correspondence have on our customers.

Given his comprehension of the impacts of the vagus nerve, Polyvagal theory creator takes note of that, expanding that breathing out longer than breathing in for a while initiates the parasympathetic sensory system. Being a clarinet player in his childhood and he recollects the impact of the breath designs required to play that instrument.

As a moving advisor, I am mindful that expanding breathes out helps customers who are stuck in types of fight-or-flight reaction to move into a feeling of security. For customers stuck in some type of shutdown, I have discovered that cognizant breathwork can mix the fight-or-flight reaction. At the point when this happens, the fight-or-flight vitality should be released through development for customers to discover a feeling of wellbeing. For example, these customers may need to run set up or punch a pad. The chain of importance of barrier framework working clarifies these remedial procedures.

Respiratory sinus arrhythmia is a decent file of ventral vagal working. This implies we currently have techniques to think about the viability of body treatments and expressive expressions treatments.

Importance Of Polyvagal Theory In The Treatment Of Nervous Problems

What follows is a brief story of how the polyvagal hypothesis was utilized by a therapist on a customer who experienced a restorative injury during her introduction to the world.

The customer, whom I have seen for quite a while, portrayed inclination extremely sluggish and recognized experiencing issues getting to our session on this day. Her therapist had recommended her Zoloft as a method for treating uneasiness blended by the introduction of her little girl's first youngster. The customer and I had recently standardized her tension as an injury reaction.

During the previous years when she comes to see me, this customer had endeavored suicide, which brought about the restorative methodology that adds to her injury. Through our work, she has come to comprehend that the fits of anxiety she has when in contained circumstances are likewise injury reactions. She has lived quite a bit of her life in unending fight-or-flight reaction mode.

On this day, she was assuaged to be less passionate, however, she dreaded the tiredness that went with Zoloft's assistance in quieting her fight-or-flight sensations. I considered this to be of the tiredness as a dread of the dorsal vagal shutdown. We talked about the likelihood that this tiredness could permit her another sort of initiation. I inquired as to whether she might want to do some expressive workmanship that would permit delicate, expressive development. She shivered, naming her inclination for less abstract things.

We discussed the presence of a sort of aliveness that still has a sense of security. We discussed the plausibility of existing in an energetic spot where there is no good and bad, just inclination. We recognized that since her introduction to the world, she and her folks had expected that her wellbeing would bomb once more. This condition where she had grown up had upheld sensory system working intended forever compromising circumstances. With the Zoloft quieting her fight-or-flight initiation, I proposed that maybe she could investigate some more settled, progressively perky sorts of emotional encounters.

"It feels like you are attempting to make an alternate me," she reacted. I recognized that it might seem as though I were suspecting she could be somebody she wasn't. In any case, I clarified that what I was proposing was simply the likelihood that she could be in an alternate manner.

The customer revealed to me she had another book on grandparenting that contained a section on the play. She said she would think about understanding it. Simultaneously, she said that she probably wouldn't have the option to endure the Zoloft and might need to get off of it. In any case, the possibility of this unique, increasingly lively method for being has been acquainted with her and, for a minute or two, experienced.

As advocates outfitted with a polyvagal hypothesis, we can picture the barrier instrument chain of command. We can perceive shifts from fight or-trip to shutdown when customers feel caught. We can likewise perceive the development from shutdown into fight-or-flight that offers a potential move into social commitment science if and when the customer can increase a feeling of wellbeing.

Before the polyvagal hypothesis, most guides could likely perceive fight-or-flight and shutdown practices. They could most likely detect a contrast between protection reactions intended forever compromising circumstances and reactions that portray what the polyvagal creator calls the social commitment framework. Polyvagal hypothesis develops that mindfulness with the information that energetic excitement and therapeutic give up have a one of a kind sensory system impact.

Most advocates acknowledge mind science, however, may think that its hard to picture how to utilize the data. Because of the polyvagal hypothesis' explanation of the job of the central part of the vagus nerve, we presently have a guide to direct us.

Chapter 2 Introduction to Stress

Behavioral medicine and health psychology are two approaches to understanding stress and its relationship to mental and physical health.

To a scientist, a stressor will be any action or event that places special physical or psychological demands on a person and can be anything that can unbalance an individual's equilibrium.

Stress at times emanates from a major life change, some other times a built-in part of one's daily life—a constant and unconscious background experience, like the noise of a city, or the daily chore of driving a car.

When we experience stress, our body responds with an unconscious preparation for an immediate defensive response.

Prolonged psychological stress may negatively impact health, and has been cited as a factor in cognitive impairment with aging, depressive illness, and expression of disease.

Given that pressure has been connected as a co-factor in 95% or all disease forms, a cornerstone of all-encompassing, elective wellbeing and recuperating is figuring out how to viably oversee pressure. This learning procedure starts with perceiving or recognizing four explicit sorts of pressure influencing you and how these stressors (that is, the thing that requests a change from you) are appearing or showing as manifestations throughout your life.

Stress is classified under four major categories: physical stress, psychological stress, psychosocial stress, and psycho-spiritual stress.

Physical Stress: injury (damage, contamination, medical procedure), exceptional physical work/over-effort, ecological contamination (pesticides, herbicides, poisons, substantial metals, insufficient light, radiation, commotion, electromagnetic fields), sickness (viral, bacterial, or contagious operators), weakness, lacking oxygen supply, hypoglycemia I(low glucose), hormonal and additionally biochemical lopsided characteristics, dietary pressure (nourishing inadequacies, nourishment hypersensitivities and sensitivities, undesirable dietary patterns), parchedness, substance misuse, dental difficulties, and musculoskeletal misalignments/awkward nature.

Psychological Stress: passionate pressure (feelings of hatred, fears, disappointment, misery, outrage, pain/mourning), subjective stress (data over-burden, quickened feeling of time, stress, blame, disgrace, envy, obstruction, connections, self-analysis, self-hatred, unworkable hairsplitting, nervousness, alarm assaults, not feeling like yourself, not feeling like things are genuine, and a feeling of being crazy/not being in charge), and perceptual pressure (convictions, jobs, stories, frames of mind, world view).

Psycho-social Stress: relationship/marriage challenges (accomplice, kin, youngsters, family, manager, colleagues, business), absence of social help, absence of assets for satisfactory endurance, loss of work/speculations/investment funds, loss of friends and family, chapter 11, home dispossession, and segregation.

Psycho-spiritual Stress: An emergency of qualities, which means, and reason; dreary endeavoring (rather than gainful, fulfilling, significant and satisfying work; and a misalignment within one's center otherworldly convictions.

By and large, inappropriately or incapably oversaw pressure as a rule negatively affects the body. At the point when stress-related sentiments, states of mind, feelings are driven into the body, the soma, this is generally named psychosomatic or psychogenic sickness, including cerebral pains, heart palpitations, physical/subjective/passionate agony and enduring, tightened throat and shallow, contracted breathing, damp palms, weakness, queasiness, tension, sensitivities, asthma, immune system disorders identified with an ineffectual working of the insusceptible framework, (hypertension), and gastrointestinal aggravations, for example, loose bowels, resentful stomach, duodenal ulcers, and esophageal reflux disorder.

Delayed pressure can bring about smothered insusceptible capacity, expanded helplessness to irresistible and invulnerable related illnesses and malignant growth. Passionate pressure can likewise bring about hormonal irregular characteristics (adrenal, pituitary, thyroid, etcetera) that further meddle with sound resistant working.

Intellectual: Anxious contemplations, dreadful expectation, poor focus, trouble with memory.

Enthusiastic: Feelings of pressure, crabbiness, fretfulness, stresses, powerlessness to unwind, gloom.

Conduct: Avoidance of errands; rest issues; trouble in finishing work assignments; squirming; tremors; stressed face; holding clench hands; crying; changes in drinking, eating, or smoking practices.

Physiological: Stiff or tense muscles, granulating teeth, perspiring, strain cerebral pains, blackout emotions, gagging feeling, trouble in gulping, stomachache, queasiness, spewing, slackening of guts, obstruction, recurrence, and desperation of pee, loss of enthusiasm for sex, tiredness, precariousness or tremors, weight reduction or addition, familiarity with heartbeat.

Social: Some individuals in distressing occasions will in general search out others to be with. Others pull back under pressure. Additionally, the nature of connections can change when an individual is under pressure.

Types Of Stress

Stress can be characterized as a change that causes physical, passionate or mental strain. In any case, not a wide range of pressure is destructive or even negative. Stressors can be either negative or positive. Distress, or negative stress, is thought to be extreme, overwhelming, and out of a person's control, while eustress, or positive stress, can be motivating and helpful.

Here are the various kinds of stress:

- Eustress
- Distress
- Acute Stress
- Episodic Acute Stress
- Chronic Stress

What Is Eustress?
If the possibility of positive pressure is different from you, you're not the only one. The greater part of us likens all worry with negative encounters.

A clinical specialist advised that we seldom consider pressure a positive thing, however, eustress is only that — positive pressure. "Energizing or distressing occasions cause a synthetic reaction in the body," he clarified. Eustress is typically a result of nerves, which can be expedited when looked with a fun test. He says this is significant because, without eustress, our prosperity can endure. "Eustress encourages us remain roused, progress in the direction of objectives, and like life," he included.

What makes eustress positive stress?

As far as contrary energies, misery and eustress are on either end of the range. Dissimilar to eustress, misery can make you feel overpowered because your assets (physically, intellectually, inwardly) are insufficient to fulfill the needs you're confronting. Authorized proficient advocator, says this kind of negative pressure can prompt nervousness, sorrow, and a lessening in execution.

Working and living outside of our usual range of familiarity is something to be thankful for. It's the point at which we feel overpowered that pressure can turn negative. That is the thing that makes eustress such a significant piece of our general wellbeing. Eustress produces positive sentiments of fervor, satisfaction, which means, fulfillment, and prosperity. He clarifies that eustress is acceptable because you feel certain, satisfactory, and invigorated by the test you experience from the stressor.

Another clinician discussed that eustress is about adequately testing yourself without consuming every one of your assets. This sort of stress enables you to develop in three zones:

Inwardly, eustress can bring about positive sentiments of satisfaction, motivation, inspiration, and stream.

Mentally, eustress causes us to construct our self-adequacy, independence, and strength.

Physically, eustress causes us to construct our body (e.g., by finishing a difficult exercise).

What are a few instances of eustress?

You can discover eustress in all aspects of your life. From work and relational connections to home and family connections, chances to encounter positive pressure are bounteous.

He also shares a few different ways you may see eustress appear in your life:

How eustress works?

A case of eustress at work is taking on another undertaking that urges you to use existing qualities (which can be extraordinarily invigorating) and expects you to sharpen existing abilities or adopt new ones.

Business-related activities will possibly drive eustress on the off chance that they're testing yet sensible. On the off chance that cutoff times are ridiculously tight, you're shuffling various tasks (an unreasonable outstanding task at hand), or working with a dangerous group culture, you're bound to encounter trouble and the negative results that accompany it.

Defining testing objectives around your inclinations or interests is another case of eustress. As people, we have an inborn capacity to learn. Adapting new things can be testing. What's more, developing aptitude in a region doesn't occur in a straight line.

There's ordinarily that learning stage where you might be completely horrendous. Yet, you're gaining from those missteps. As you start seeing little successes and keep on building self-viability, you're propelled to keep learning and improving.

Eustress and travel

Voyaging is inalienably distressing, particularly when you're investigating a faraway spot with an alternate language and customs.

Simultaneously, you're drenching yourself in another and fascinating spot, with different nourishments to appreciate, new places to see, and an entire culture to understand.

Albeit unpleasant, voyaging is an enlightening encounter for some individuals that are seen decidedly.

Eustress and physical molding

Physically, eustress is exemplified by testing your body (e.g., lifting loads) to support development (for this situation, quality, stamina, and muscle development).

In the rec center or out on a mobile way, you may be sticking out to your tunes and completely zoned into your exercise. You may not understand how depleting the work has become because you're up to speed at the time.

What are approaches to remember progressively positive worry for your life?

There's a decent possibility you as of now remember positive worry for your life. In any case, in case you're searching for approaches to make eustress a piece of your consistently.

Gain some new useful knowledge consistently, regardless of whether enormous or little.

Propel yourself outside of your usual range of familiarity at work. This may mean taking on another duty or building up another ability.

Figure out how to set objectives (individual and expert) that are testing and sensible. Keep tabs on your development to consider yourself responsible.

Find out about more approaches to oversee negative pressure and improve your wellbeing and mindset.

Stress, regardless of whether positive or negative, is an ordinary piece of life. We might not have authority over a portion of the negative pressure we experience, yet we can search for approaches to incorporate more eustress in our life.

How Your Body Responds To Stress

Stress can trigger the body's reaction to an apparent risk or peril, known as the fight-or-flight response.

During this response, certain hormones like adrenaline and cortisol are discharged. This speeds the pulse, eases back absorption, shunts bloodstream to significant muscle gatherings, and changes different other autonomic anxious capacities, giving the body an explosion of vitality and quality.

Initially named for its capacity to empower us to physically fight or flee when looked with peril, it's currently initiated in circumstances where neither one of the responses is suitable—like in rush hour gridlock or during an upsetting day at work.

At the point when the apparent danger is gone, frameworks are intended to come back to ordinary capacity employing the unwinding response. But in instances of incessant pressure, the unwinding reactions don't happen regularly enough, and being in a close consistent condition of fight-or-flight can make harm the body.

Stress can likewise prompt some undesirable propensities that negatively affect your wellbeing. For instance, numerous individuals adapt to worry by eating excessively or by smoking. These undesirable propensities harm the body and make more concerning issues in the long-term.3

The Impact of Stress on Your Health

The association between your brain and body is evident when you analyze the effect pressure has on your life. Learning about worried over a relationship, cash, or your living circumstance can make physical medical problems.

The reverse is additionally valid. Medical issues, regardless of whether you're managing hypertension or you have diabetes, will likewise influence your feeling of anxiety and your psychological well-being.

At the point when your mind encounters high degrees of stress, your body responds in like manner.

Genuine intense pressure, such as being engaged with a catastrophic event or getting into a verbal fight, can trigger coronary failures, arrhythmias, and even unexpected demise. Notwithstanding, this happens generally in people who as of now have heart diseases.

Incessant pressure can seriously affect your wellbeing also. On the off chance that you experience interminable pressure, your autonomic sensory system will be overactive, which is probably going to harm your body.

The principal side effects are generally gentle, as interminable migraines and expanded vulnerability to colds. With more introduction to incessant pressure, be that as it may, progressively genuine medical issues may create. They incorporate, yet are not constrained to:

Stress-Influenced Conditions

- Diabetes
- Male pattern baldness
- Coronary illness
- Hyperthyroidism
- Weight
- Sexual brokenness
- Tooth and gum illness
- Ulcers

Stress likewise causes significant damage. While some pressure may deliver sentiments of gentle tension or dissatisfaction, delayed pressure can prompt burnout, uneasiness issue, and despondency. One must find ways to effectively combat stress, as when this can be done, there would be great improvement in health level.

Figuring out how to Manage Stress

Regardless of the way that weight is certain, it might be reasonable. Right, when you fathom the cost it figures out how to fight pressure, you can accept accountability for your prosperity and diminishing the impact pressure has on your life. The going with articles on this journey will help you with perceiving how stress impacts you.

It will moreover help you in perceiving the best weight decline frameworks that will work for you and it will help with preventing burnout. Here's a glance at what you'll understand: Perceive the Signs of Burnout Significant degrees of weight may put you at a high peril of burnout. Burnout can leave you feeling exhausted and disconnected about your activity.?

Luckily, there are steps you can take to prevent and address burnout if you see the signs. How Stress Impacts Weight Stress can make weight changes in a combination of ways. A portion of the time it impacts hunger. At various events, it can impact processing and hormones to the point that it ends up being too difficult to even think about evening consider dealing with your weight, paying little mind to your diet.

How Exercise Reduces Stress

Physical action affects your cerebrum and your body greatly. Regardless of whether you appreciate Tai Chi or you need to start running, practice lessens pressure and improves numerous manifestations related to mental illness.

Compelling Ways to Manage Stress

In spite of the fact that there's a great deal of discussion about the significance of overseeing pressure, the vast majority aren't certain how to do it. It's essential to have a tool kit loaded up with pressure decrease devices that assist you with combatting pressure viably.

Set up a Self-Care Routine

Consolidating normal self-care exercises into your day by day life is basic to stretch administration. Figure out how to deal with your brain, body, and soul and find how to prepare yourself to live your best life.

Carry on with a More Mindful Life

Care isn't simply something you practice for 10 minutes every day. It can likewise be a lifestyle.

Discover how to live more cautiously reliably so you can end up being progressively alert and discerning for an inconceivable length.

Distress: A negative reaction to a stressor, which is described by feeling wild, overpowered, and sad. wellbeing brain research: A control worried about seeing how organic, mental, natural, and social components are associated with physical wellbeing and the anticipation of ailment.

stressor: A natural condition or impact that anxieties (i.e., causes worry for) a living being.

Eustress: A positive reaction to a stressor, which can rely upon one's present sentiments of control, attractive quality, area, and timing. Stress can be characterized from multiple points of view, contingent upon the individual encountering it and the viewpoint used to get it. One essential meaning of pressure is "a mental inclination of strain and weight."

Social medication and wellbeing brain research are two ways to deal with breaking down and talking about pressure. To researchers, a stressor is any activity or circumstance that spots exceptional physical or mental requests upon an individual, and can be whatever can unbalance the person's harmony.

Stress may originate from a significant life change, or it might be a work in part of one's day by day life; it very well may be a steady and oblivious foundation experience, similar to the clamor of a city, or the day by day task of driving a vehicle. At the point when individuals are looked with requests to which they feel unfit to satisfactorily react, they are spurred to plan something to change the circumstance.

The idea of this reaction relies upon a blend of various variables, including the degree of the interest, the individual attributes and adapting assets of the individual, the requirements on the individual attempting to adapt, and the help got from others.

Distress and Eustress

Stress can be either positive (eustress) or negative (trouble). Significantly, the body itself can't physically perceive between trouble or eustress; the qualification is reliant on the experience of the individual encountering the pressure. Misery, or adverse pressure, has pessimistic ramifications and is normally seen to be possibly overpowering and out of an individual's control. Calamities, diseases, and mishaps will, in general, be the focal point of negative pressure.

Eustress, or positive worry, then again, is the positive enthusiastic or subjective reaction to stretch that is solid; it gives a sentiment of satisfaction or joy. Eustress has a positive connection with life fulfillment and expectation since it cultivates challenge and inspiration toward an objective. Any occasion can cause either trouble or eustress, contingent upon how the individual deciphers the data.

For instance, horrendous get-togethers may cause extraordinary misery, yet in addition, eustress as versatility, adapting and encouraging a feeling of the social network.

DEFINITION OF DISTRESS
There are various definitions of Distress. Most definitions portray trouble as an aversive, negative state in which adapting and adjustment forms neglect to restore a living being to physiological or potentially mental homeostasis. Movement into the maladaptive state might be because of an extreme or delayed stressor or numerous total unpleasant put-down with pernicious impacts on the creature's welfare. Trouble can follow both intense and interminable pressure, given that the body's natural

capacities are adequately modified and its ways of dealing with stress overpowered.

The progress of worry to trouble relies upon a few components. Of clear significance are stressor length and power, both of which are probably going to deliver social or physical indications of pain. For instance, the transient restriction doesn't cause stamped issues in adjustment, while delayed limitation can bring about social or physiological misery some of the time communicated by vocalization or gastric ulcers. Moreover, consistency and controllability (i.e., the capacity of the creature to control its condition) are significant determinants in the change of worry to trouble. Various investigations show that, in creatures that can foresee the beginning of an upsetting upgrade or control its span, the conduct and physiological effects of stressor presentation are lessened. Prominent among these examinations are discoveries that rodents presented to inevitable stun grow clear indications of misery, though burdened rodents that can end stun introduction don't, notwithstanding subjection to a similar force and span of stun understanding.

Besides, the pressure reaction may initiate lacking or improper changes in the social and physiologic control frameworks (noted above) or deficient or unfortunate reactions to their yield signals. For instance, constant social subjection has been appeared to inspire conduct withdrawal, delayed adjustments in the hypothalamic-pituitary-adrenal (HPA) pivot yield, and resulting immunosuppression, all of which block successful adapting and adjustment. Further examinations have indicated that in incessant trouble states, for example, despondency, the glucocorticoid criticism frameworks come up short. Therefore, if stress reactions themselves neglect to fittingly adapt or create effective adjustment they might be not simply incapable however effectively malicious. For instance, while corticosteroid reactions are basic for the adjustment procedure, checked or delayed hypersecretion can deliver articulated metabolic and insusceptible brokenness.

Acute Stress

Acute pressure is the sort of stress that quickly unsettles you. This is the kind of stress that goes ahead rapidly and regularly surprisingly and does not keep going excessively long, yet requires a reaction and startles you up somewhat, relative to a contention with a person in your life, or a test for which you don't feel sufficiently prepared for.

There are a few unique sorts of pressure, and not every one of them is fundamentally unfortunate.

Intense pressure is one of the least harming kinds of stress, which is acceptable in light of the fact that it is likewise the most widely recognized sort. We experience intense pressure on numerous occasions for the duration of the day. Intense pressure is experienced as a quickly seen risk, either physical, enthusiastic or mental. These dangers don't should be strongly undermining—they can be mellow stressors like a morning timer going off, another task at work, or even a telephone call that should be replied when you're unwinding on the love seat and your telephone is over the room.

Intense pressure can likewise be increasingly genuine, such as being pulled over for speeding, getting into contention with a companion, or stepping through an exam. The risk can be genuine or envisioned; it's the impression of danger that triggers the pressure reaction. During an intense pressure reaction, the autonomic sensory system is actuated and the body encounters expanded degrees of cortisol, adrenaline and different hormones that produce an expanded pulse, animated breathing rate, and more severe hypertension.

Blood is shunted from the furthest points to the large muscles, setting up the body to battle or flee. This is otherwise called the battle or-flight reaction. Intense pressure can be overseen effectively on the grounds that it happens and afterward it's finished. It doesn't expedite the cost wellbeing that accompanies incessant pressure since it is conceivable and moderately simple to recuperate from intense pressure—straightforward unwinding procedures can work rapidly of your pressure reaction doesn't resolve into an unwinding reaction all alone.

Rehashed occasions of intense pressure, be that as it may, can bring to a greater degree a cost. Either various occasions of various intense stressors (a progression of irrelevant unpleasant occasions) or rehashed events of similar intense stressors (encountering a similar pressure more than once) can indicate a condition of interminable pressure where the body's pressure reaction is continually activated.

Along these lines, it's critical to have pressure on the board plan. The accompanying advances can lessen the odds of having your intense stressors mean increasingly critical degrees of stress.

Acute Stress Relief Techniques

Your body's pressure reaction is activated with intense pressure, however, you can switch it with speedy unwinding systems, and afterward return to your day feeling less focused on once more. These pressure relief techniques can assist you with relaxing and all the more rapidly recoup you from intense pressure.

Cutting down on the little things that repeatedly stress you— your tolerations—can minimize your overall stress levels. You can also take other steps to minimize lifestyle stress. You can't eliminate all stress (nor would you want to), but you can cut out stress where possible and this can really add up.

Learn Relaxation Techniques That Work for You

This means finding ways to relax your body and calm your mind. You can't always predict the stressors in your life, but you can reverse your stress response after you encounter these stressors.

Adopt Resilience-Building Habits

Yes, certain habits can build resilience toward stress. These include meditation, exercise, and more. Taking on one of these habits (or several) can really help you to manage acute stress as well as chronic stress.

Breathing Exercises: Great for intense pressure since they work rapidly.

Subjective Reframing: Learn to change the manner in which you take a gander at the circumstance to deal with your feelings of anxiety.

Dynamic Muscle Relaxation: Like breathing activities, PMR will give you a minute to refocus and quiet down.

Smaller than usual Meditation: Take breathing activities above and beyond with this snappy, 5-minute contemplation method to quiet down at the time.

What Is Chronic Stress?

Incessant pressure results from a condition of progressing physiological excitement. This happens when the body encounters stressors with such recurrence or power that the autonomic sensory system doesn't have a satisfactory opportunity to actuate the unwinding reaction all the time.

This implies the body stays in a steady condition of physiological excitement. It influences for all intents and purposes each framework in the body, either straightforwardly or in a roundabout way. We were worked to deal with intense pressure, which is fleeting, however not ceaseless pressure, which is consistent over an extensive stretch of time.

Chronic pressure is the kind of stress that will, in general, happen all the time. This sort of stress may leave you feeling depleted, and can prompt burnout if it's not successfully overseen. This is on the grounds that, when the pressure reaction is incessantly activated and the body isn't taken back to a casual state before the following influx of stress hits, the body can remain activated uncertainly.

Chronic pressure can prompt a large group of medical problems, including cardiovascular disease, gastrointestinal issues, uneasiness, despondency, and a large group of different conditions. This is the reason it is essential to adequately oversee incessant pressure. Dealing with this sort of stress regularly requires a mix approach, with some momentary pressure relievers (like those for intense pressure), and some extended pressure help propensities that calm generally speaking pressure. (Distinctive feeling centered adapting procedures and arrangement centered adapting strategies are significant too.)

The accompanying extended propensities can assist you with bettering oversee general pressure that you may feel from the interminable stressors throughout your life.

Exercise Regularly: Exercise and stress the board is firmly connected for a few reasons.

Keep up a Healthy Diet: Fueling your body well can help with by and large feelings of anxiety on the grounds that your whole framework will work better.

Develop Supportive Relationships: Having a strong emotionally supportive network is an urgent method for dealing with stress.

Contemplate Regularly: While brisk reflections are extraordinary for managing intense pressure, an ordinary contemplation practice will help assemble your general strength to push.

Tune in to Music: Music can go about as a great, stress-diminishing setting to regular errands.

Passionate Stress

Hit with melancholy

The agony of enthusiastic pressure can hit more enthusiastically than some different sorts of pressure. For instance, the pressure that originates from a tangled relationship will, in general, bring a more noteworthy physical response and a more grounded feeling of trouble than the pressure that originates from being occupied at work.

Hence, it is imperative to have the option to oversee enthusiastic worry in powerful manners. Techniques that help you to process, diffuse, and manufacture flexibility toward passionate pressure would all be able to function admirably, and various methodologies can work in various circumstances. Here are a few different ways to oversee passionate pressure.

Write in a Journal: There are a few diverse journaling procedures to attempt, all with benefits.

Converse with a Friend: Learn about the few unique kinds of social help companions can offer you.

Practice Mindfulness: Mindfulness can help keep you established right now.

Doing combating Burnout

Lady with heaps of papers around her work area

Burnout

Burnout is the consequence of the delayed constant worry of circumstances that leave individuals feeling an absence of control in their lives. Certain states of a vocation can make a more serious danger of burnout, including a significant level of requests, yet in addition, vague desires, absence of acknowledgment for accomplishments, and an elevated level of danger of negative outcomes when slip-ups are made.

When you arrive at a condition of burnout, it is hard to keep up inspiration to work and achieve what you have to achieve, and you can feel constantly overpowered. Notwithstanding the techniques that function admirably for interminable pressure and passionate pressure, the accompanying systems can assist you with coming back from a condition of burnout—or forestall it totally.

Take Some Time Off: If you never take as much time as is needed, here's the reason you should begin.

Get More Laughter into Your Life: Laughter can prompt better generally speaking wellbeing and bring satisfaction into your day.

Enjoy Hobbies: Don't hold up until your life quiets down to take part in your leisure activities.

Get More Enjoyment Out of Your Current Job: If you found in work you don't adore, all isn't lost. Figure out how to make your activity additionally satisfying.

Make the most of Your Weekends: Learn how to bring a portion of your end of the week into your workweek for less pressure.

Causes of burnout

This sort of incessant pressure reaction happens very regularly from our cutting edge way of life. Everything from high-forced occupations to forlornness to occupied traffic can keep the body in a condition of the apparent risk and ceaseless pressure.

For this situation, our fight or-flight reaction, which was intended to assist us with battling a couple of perilous circumstances scattered over a significant stretch (like being assaulted by a bear now and again), can wear out our bodies and cause us to turn out to be sick, either physically or inwardly.

Truth be told, it's evaluated that up to 90% of specialist's visits are for conditions in which stress assumes a job! That is the reason it is so critical to learn pressure the executive's methods and make a sound way of life changes to protect yourself from the negative effect of incessant pressure.

Instances of Acute versus Chronic Stress

Numerous life occasions cause both intense and incessant pressure. To place the two into point of view, here are a couple of models.

Chronic Stress Is Short-Term

Chronic pressure can happen when you get into a fender bender. You do not just need to manage police reports, insurance agencies and surveying the harm to yourself and your vehicle, however you have to discover how to get the opportunity to function the following day.

The greater part of these issues will be turned out inside seven days (perhaps up to a month) and soon after the mishap, your underlying pressure is diminished on the grounds that the circumstance is leveled out. In any event, you are sheltered!

Another model is the point at which you are chipping away at a significant undertaking for work. You put in extended periods of time and have a tight and approaching cutoff time. This can cause numerous unpleasant days as you calibrate the entirety of the subtleties. Nonetheless, when the task is submitted, you can unwind.

For this situation, your pressure may have helped you perform better on the grounds that not all pressure is awful.

Interminable Stress Is Long-Term

Then again, if your family is battling monetarily or with a serious ailment, the pressure can get interminable. Somebody in your home will most likely be unable to work, bills are accumulating and your house is approaching dispossession and this can leave you worried for a considerable length of time or even a year or more.

Your steady stress wears out your body, making you feel worn out and on edge. You might be working harder than at any other time to make a decent living and settle on unfortunate decisions about nourishment and exercise, which can aggravate you feel even. This can prompt genuine melancholy among other wellbeing concerns.

We can likewise have incessant pressure identified with work. Numerous occupations require a ton out from us and it can regularly feel like you never get a break or are constantly constrained to perform.

Staying at work past 40 hours, steady travel and high-pressure business relations can keep your body in a consistent condition of fervor, in any event, when you return home to your family. This can likewise add to the mileage on your body and consistent pressure can add to genuine medical problems like coronary illness or lead to respiratory failure.

On the off chance that You Are Experiencing Chronic Stress

It is imperative to start utilizing pressure the board methods as ahead of schedule as conceivable when you perceive interminable worry in your life. This works for a couple of reasons.

Quick-acting pressure relievers can switch the pressure reaction so your body gets an opportunity to recuperate and your psyche gets an opportunity to move toward issues from a proactive position instead of to respond from a pushed or even terrified point of view. At the point when you're settling on decisions from an increasingly loose and sure spot, you will in general settle on decisions that are more in accordance with your eventual benefits and abstain from making more worry for yourself.

Longer-term solid propensities can likewise be essential to actualize on the grounds that they can manufacture flexibility and give you opportunities to take a break from weight all the time. This can assist you with keeping from remaining focused so always that you don't understand how focused on you are, which can prevent you from finding a way to lessen the worry in your life. It can likewise spare you from the more negative impacts of incessant pressure. Probably the best propensities incorporate exercise, reflection, and journaling, as they have been appeared to elevate flexibility to push

Changing how you react to pressure can help also. By making changes to lessen the distressing circumstances you face (saying no more regularly, for instance) and by changing the manner in which you take a gander at the circumstances you face (helping yourself to remember the assets you can utilize and the quality you have) can both assistance. Moving toward worry from a proactive position can help decrease interminable pressure.

Episodic Acute Stress Disorder
This sort of stress regularly influences the sort of individuals that others allude to as "Type A." Patients experience outsized worry in response to improvements. Now and again, the pressure is simply the aftereffect of ridiculous desires. Like with intense pressure issue, the

feelings are extraordinary and not interminable. In any case, the triggers are unique.

What is Episodic Acute Stress Disorder?

Somebody with verbose intense pressure encounters extraordinary pressure and decisive sentiments in light of moderately everyday stressors. Despite the fact that others may call these individuals "excessively emotional," they simply don't comprehend that Episodic Acute Stress Disorder is a genuine ailment. Moreover, the individual with the confusion feels certifiable pressure that may make them think these circumstances are last chance.

For instance, somebody may miss a cutoff time at work and quickly start having an outsized response. Regardless of whether the individual's manager isn't excessively furious, the patient may begin feeling that she will lose her employment, become destitute, and bite the dust in the city. To her, the frenzy is a sensible response, however, as a general rule, it is harming her.

Indications of Episodic Acute Stress Disorder

It tends to be hard for individuals with this issue to get the treatment they need since they feel just as the pressure is the correct response and their emotionally supportive network may expel the side effects. A few indications of this disorder include uncontrolled displeasure, Fast heartbeat, Fit of anxiety, Indigestion and other gastrointestinal difficulties, Solid torment and snugness. If these Left untreated, this issue can prompt bigger medical issues, including Coronary illness, cerebral pains, Hypertension

Way of life changes, treatment, and drugs would all be able to be a piece of a treatment plan for Episodic Acute Stress Disorder. Specialists may suggest a way of life changes, for example, changing employments or beginning a physical exercise schedule. CBT can assist patients with figuring out how to respond to triggers strongly. The drug can help on those occasions when the pressure is a lot for the patient to deal with.

Stress and Health

Prolonged mental pressure may contrarily affect wellbeing, and has been referred to as a factor in intellectual debilitation with maturing, burdensome sickness, and articulation of ailment. There is proof that specific negative mental states, (for example, misery, and uneasiness) can legitimately influence physical invulnerability through the creation of stress hormones, for example, catecholamines and glucocorticoids. Stress the board is the utilization of techniques to either diminish pressure or increment resilience to push.

Unwinding procedures are physical techniques used to assuage pressure. Mental techniques incorporate psychological treatment, reflection, and positive reasoning, which work by lessening the reaction to stretch. Improving pertinent aptitudes, for example, critical thinking and time-the board abilities decrease

64

vulnerability and constructs certainty, which additionally lessens the response to negative pressure causing circumstances in which those aptitudes are appropriate. Athletic challenge: Competing in athletic occasions frequently prompts eustress.

How the Body Responds to Stress

The right responds to stress is very important, this is so essential when it comes to our response to the body stress. When given pressure, the body reacts by discharging hormones that will set it up for the battle or flight reaction. The connections of endocrine hormones that have developed to settle the body's an inside condition can be disturbed by pressure. The sympathetic sensory system controls the pressure reaction employing the nerve center.

The hormones epinephrine (otherwise called adrenaline) and norepinephrine (otherwise called noradrenaline) are discharged by the adrenal medulla. Epinephrine and norepinephrine increment blood glucose levels by invigorating the liver and skeletal muscles to separate glycogen and by animating glucose discharge by liver cells. Epinephrine and norepinephrine are by and large called catecholamine. Stressors are upgrades that disturb homeostasis.

Despite the fact that our bodies can react to and manage to worry, for the time being, extended presentation to stretch hormones can have hindering impacts. catecholamine: Any of a class of fragrant amines got from pyrocatechol that are hormones delivered by the adrenal organ. homeostasis: The capacity of a framework or living being to alter its inner condition to keep up a steady balance, for example, the capacity of warm-blooded creatures to keep up a consistent temperature.

nerve center: The district of the forebrain underneath the thalamus, framing the basal bit of the diencephalon; controls internal heat level and some metabolic procedures, and oversees the autonomic sensory system. The body reacts to worry in certain physiological manners. At the point when a risk or peril is seen, the body reacts by discharging hormones that will set it up for the fight-or-flight reaction.

The fundamental physiological structure engaged with this reaction is known as the HPA (hypothalamic–pituitary organ – adrenal organ) hub. Such communications of the endocrine hormones have developed to guarantee that the body's inward condition stays stable; be that as it may, stress can disturb this solidness. Upgrades that disturb homeostasis along these lines are known as stressors.

The Fight-or-Flight Response

When our bodies are looked with a stressor—any trigger that prompts a pressure reaction—certain physical procedures occur. The body responds in a crude sense to what it sees as approaching threat in what is informally named the battle or-flight reaction (some of the time "battle flight-or-freeze"). Blood from your skin, organs, and furthest points is coordinated to the mind and bigger muscles in arrangement to battle the looming risk or escape from it.

Furthermore, your faculties (particularly vision and hearing) are elevated, glucose and unsaturated fats are discharged into the circulation system for vitality, and your resistant and stomach related frameworks everything except shut down to give you the fundamental vitality to battle the stressor. The HPA pivot arranges all these physiological changes. Wellbeing brain research centers around this physical response and what it implies for an individual's wellbeing and prosperity.

Recognizable Symptoms of Stress delivers various side effects that differ as per individual, circumstance, and seriousness. Issues coming about because of stress remember decrease for physical wellbeing or emotional wellness, a feeling of being overpowered, sentiments of tension, by and large crabbiness, frailty, anxiety, social withdrawal, loss of hunger, discouragement, alarm assaults, depletion, high or low pulse, skin ejections or rashes, a sleeping disorder, absence of sexual want (sexual brokenness), headache, gastrointestinal challenges (clogging or loose bowels), heart issues, and menstrual manifestations.

Stress and the body: This chart shows the impacts of weight on different parts and frameworks of the body.

The HPA Axis

The hypothalamic-pituitary-adrenal hub (HPA axis) is a perplexing arrangement of direct impacts and input co-operations among three endocrine organs: the nerve center, the pituitary organ, and the adrenal organs.

The HPA hub is a significant piece of the neuroendocrine framework that, in addition to other things, controls responses to stretch. The HPA framework responds inside an individual's cerebrum, and it discharges the hormone cortisol from the adrenal organ when an individual is presented to a stressor. Cortisol is well on the way to be actuated when an individual is put in a circumstance to be socially judged or assessed, and in this manner under outrageous degrees of stress.

Higher and increasingly drawn-out degrees of cortisol in the circulation system is found in those experiencing constant pressure. The nerve center produces Corticotropin-Releasing Hormone (CRH), which initiates Adrenocorticotropic Hormone (ACTH) creation in the Anterior Pituitary, which enacts Cortisol generation in the Adrenal Cortex. The Cortisol impacts negative criticism of the Hypothalamus and the Anterior Pituitary.

The pressure reaction: The sympathetic sensory system manages the pressure reaction by means of the nerve center. In spite of the fact that our bodies can react to and manage to worry, for the time being, extended introduction to push hormones can have unfavorable impacts. For instance, it can prompt a diminishing memory work and physical execution.

This is on the grounds that glycogen holds, which give vitality in the transient reaction to stretch, are depleted following a few hours and can't meet extended vitality needs. In the event that glycogen saves were the main vitality source accessible, neural working couldn't be kept up once the stores got drained because of the sensory system's high necessity for glucose.

Stress Hormones and Sympathetic Nervous System

Coming up next are streamlined advances that an individual's sensory system experiences when it manages an unpleasant circumstance: Blood from the skin, inner organs, and limits, is coordinated to the mind and huge muscles in anticipation of "battle" or "flight." Your faculties are uplifted, particularly vision and hearing. Glucose and unsaturated fats are constrained into the circulatory system for vitality.

The resistant and stomach related frameworks are for all intents and purposes shut down to give all the vital vitality to react to the apparent risk. The sympathetic sensory system manages the pressure reaction by means of the nerve center. Distressing boosts cause the nerve center to flag the adrenal medulla (which intervenes momentary pressure reactions) by means of nerve motivations, and the adrenal cortex (which intercedes extended pressure reactions) by means of the hormone adrenocorticotropic hormone (ACTH), which is created by the front pituitary.

At the point when given an upsetting circumstance, the body reacts by requiring the arrival of hormones that give an explosion of vitality. The hormones epinephrine (otherwise called adrenaline) and norepinephrine (otherwise called noradrenaline) are discharged by the adrenal medulla. Epinephrine and norepinephrine increment blood glucose levels by animating the liver and skeletal muscles to separate glycogen, and by invigorating glucose discharge by liver cells. Moreover, these hormones increment oxygen accessibility to cells by expanding the pulse and enlarging the bronchioles.

The hormones likewise organize bodywork by expanding blood supply to fundamental organs, for example, the heart, mind, and skeletal muscles, while confining bloodstream to organs, not in prompt need, for example, the skin, stomach related framework, and kidneys. Epinephrine and norepinephrine are all in all called catecholamine.

Test Research on the Effects of Stress

Research has discovered that keeping up great wellbeing impacts decreasing and adapting to pressure. Practices, for example, work out, contemplation, profound breathing, great dietary patterns, and getting enough rest can assist people with bettering handle pressure and stay away from adverse impacts, for example, improved probability of infection and poor processing. Tragically, stress can negatively affect the inspiration to keep up these sound practices.

While mental pressure alone has not been demonstrated to cause malignancy, delayed mental pressure may influence an individual's general wellbeing and capacity to adapt to the disease. Proof from test examines proposes that mental feelings of anxiety can influence a tumor's capacity to develop and spread. Concentrates in mice and human malignant growth cells developed in a research center have discovered that the pressure hormone norepinephrine may advance angiogenesis and metastasis.

"Angiogenesis" alludes to the advancement and arrangement of fresh recruits vessels. "Metastasis" alludes to the transference of a real capacity or disease to another piece of the body, explicitly the improvement of an auxiliary zone of sickness remote from the first sight.

Stress and Cardiovascular Disease Cardiovascular

Disease has various social hazard factors, a large number of which are identified with pressure.

Therapeutic specialists don't know precisely how stress builds the danger of coronary illness. Stress itself may be a hazard factor, or it may be the case that elevated levels of pressure exacerbate other hazard factors. Stress not just builds an individual's propensity

Chapter 3 How Does Psychological Trauma Affect the Body and the Brain?

It would take numerous volumes to talk about the mind. In this chapter, I will adhere to a review discourse of the pieces of the cerebrum that are generally applicable to the basic comprehension of injury: the cortex (the thinking focus about the cerebrum) and the Iimbic framework (the enthusiastic and endurance focus of the cerebrum).

The Cortex

Among different capacities, the cortex is the site of cognizant idea and mindfulness. Looking after consideration to our outer condition (what we see, hear, smell, and so forth.) just as our inside condition (considerations, body sensations, and feelings) requires movement in the cortex. Thinking, including the review of actualities, depiction of techniques, acknowledgment of time, understanding, etc, additionally happens in the cortex. In spite of the fact that it shifts from individual to singular, low degrees of expanded worry with the going with increment in adrenaline levels will improve mindfulness, unwavering discernment, and memory.

That is the reason espresso is such a popular demand drink at work and among college understudies: a shock of caffeine makes our memory, perceptions, and thinking forms keener. Be that as it may, past a certain (separately decided) level, expanded adrenaline will corrupt, that is, have the contrary impact on, those equivalent procedures. A most unmistakable model is seen on TV test programs.

All the more regularly than not, hopefuls dispensed with by an off-base answer will state that when watching the program at home, they never missed an answer. Why at that point would they say they were befuddled when on TV? Probably, their feelings of anxiety rose past the supportive low-adrenaline kick and surrendered to over-burden that hosed their capacity to get to data that was effectively accessible under more quiet conditions. Something very similar can occur with injury. Despite the fact that numerous survivors report a honing of recognition and thought, those with PTSD, as a rule, have an alternate encounter. In such cases, their cerebrums got over-burden with adrenaline and they were never again ready to think unmistakably as they ran, fights, or—in all probability—solidified in reaction to the awful danger. Understanding the association of the cortex with the limbic framework during low and high pressure will make this loss of cortex capacity more clear.

The Limbic System

Situated in the centerpiece of the mind between the cerebrum stem and cortex, the limbic framework is liable for our endurance. It shields us from peril in significant part by perceiving and using tactile data and afterward getting underway the defensive reactions of flight, fight, and freeze. The limbic framework evaluates the conditions of both inner and outside situations employing tactile information and moves the information to other cerebrum structures. The amygdala is the limbic structure that doles out the tactile data an enthusiastic translation and teaches the body how to react likewise.

For one, Adrenaline and noradrenaline are the recognizable names for the hormones epinephrine and norepinephrine. In the United States, the last terms are increasingly common in logical writings. Be that as it may; in Europe and somewhere else, it is the more well-known use that prevails. Since this book is composed for the two specialists and customers and will be perused on the two sides of the Atlantic Ocean, adrenaline and noradrenaline are utilized throughout. Secondly, occurrence, while trusting that your companion will show up, you may as of now be grinning as your amygdala recognizes her natural stance and walk from a separation. In sensory system time, your grinning reaction shows up well before you have intentionally perceived her face as she draws near. On the opposite finish of the range, it is likewise the amygdala that assesses tangible data (what is seen, heard, smelled, and so on.) as involving risk. In such an occurrence it will raise an alert and train the body to react in an unexpected way, to flee or plunge for spread (flight), fight off (light), or go numb or blackout (freeze).

Another structure in the limbic framework, the hippocampus, is significant for overseeing, recalling, what's more, recuperating from an injury. In addition to other things, the hippocampus registers and afterward illuminates the cortex about the time setting of an occasion. It denotes the memory of every occasion with a start, center, and end. For instance, recall a basic scene from yesterday: a supper, a telephone call, taking a shower whatever. As you infer the subtleties, notice whether you review how the episode started, what occurred during it, and afterward its finish.

As I am composing this page at this moment, I am recalling showing my older neighbor how to utilize his new cell telephone—the first he had ever possessed. It began with my thumping on his front entryway. He invited me in. At that point, we experienced the different strides of utilizing the telephone. I customized a few speed dial numbers for him and he recorded how to discover them. At that point after about 60 minutes, we were wrapped up. He stated, "Much obliged!" I said," the pleasure is all mine. Simply remember to turn it on" He let me out the entryway.

My memory of the subtleties in the grouping is because of the hippocampus carrying out its responsibility. It will, for the most part, do that for any occasion, recording and afterward telling the cortex when it began, to what extent it continued, and that it wrapped up.

Take exceptional note of that last advance of hippocampal sequencing, recording that an occasion has finished. With respect to recalling injury, this is crucially significant. Truth be told, ordinarily PTSD is the aftereffect of a hippocampus that was not ready to stamp the finish of the injury. It was always unable to tell the cortex that the injury finished. Such a disappointment of the hippocampus is actually the core of PTSD, maybe even the major cause. At the point when the hippocampus can perceive and tell the cortex that a horrible mishap has finished up, the cortex would then be able to educate the amygdala that the injury is finished. When educated, the amygdala would then be able to end its alert reaction, telling the body there is no further requirement for hypervigilance or flight, fight, or freeze. That is the thing that happens when an injury is resolved—regardless of whether at the time or in the close or far off future. The hippocampus perceives its finish and advises the cortex, which thus cautions the amygdala to stop all the guarded activity. Truth be told, it is this element of hippocampal work that makes injury recuperation conceivable. Without it, the amygdala will continue reacting as though the injury proceeds over and over and once more, which is actually what's going on when the framework falls flat and PTSD creates. All things considered, the hippocampus neglects to stamp the finish of the occasion, it can't illuminate the cortex, and the amygdala's caution persists.

Consequently, While the amygdala is resistant to the ascent in stress hormones that goes with awful pressure, the hippocampus isn't so fortunate. It is truly powerless against significant levels of pressure hormones and will quit working accurately when adrenaline and different hormones arrive at an elevated level. Stress excitement should be brought down before the hippocampus will get an opportunity to work appropriately once more.

The Twins of data Processing

A scientist recognized two pathways for the handling of tangible data. Both are speedy progressively. In any case, with regards to sensory system time, one is exceptionally quick and the other is fairly moderate. The primary, the brisk course, is by means of the amygdala and sidesteps the cortex by and large. The amygdala takes in tactile data from both inward and outer conditions (see the following area) and guides the body, how to react. For instance, hearing the voice of a friend or family member on the telephone may make you moan profoundly before you've even acknowledged what it's identity is and made proper acquaintance. The amygdala hears the voice, remembers it as comfortable and partners it with a wonderful experience. It does the same with toxic tactile data too. For instance, the smell of smoke may have your heart quickening some time before you have found the source. The amygdala enlists the smell of smoke, partners it with potential risk; and afterward readies the body for protective activity by raising the heart rate. In this snappy course of data handling, these responses are gotten underway immediately, long prior to the likelihood of any cortical contribution.

The second, more slow course uses the hippocampus to send data to the frontal cortex where it can be assessed with a cognizant idea. In the two models in the past passage, this is the ticket it would work. Hearing the voice of the adored one, the hippocampus sends data to the prefrontal cortex that makes conceivable the recognizable proof of who the individual is, the point at which you last got notification from or saw that individual, and some other indispensable data. Then again, when smelling smoke, the hippocampus would hand-off that data to the cortex where activity could be gotten underway to find the wellspring of the smoke or to verify that there is no threat either in light of the fact that the smoke has stopped or since the source was considerate. Endurance throughout everyday life, especially when managing injury, necessitates that both of these frameworks be working appropriately. Anyway, the significant levels of pressure hormones, fundamentally adrenaline, related with PTSD will in general cripple the hippocampus along the slower preparing course. At the point when excitement goes up past a certain edge, the hippocampus quits working. At the point when that occurs during an awful occurrence, the time sequencing won't be precisely recorded, on the off chance that it is recorded by any stretch of the imagination. That implies that memory of the occasion will be without structure: no start, no center, and—critically—no closure. In such an occurrence, the amygdala keeps on calling a caution as though the injury is forging ahead and on or again and once more. The cortex never got the message that it was finished, so it can't advise the amygdala to quiet down. The outcome is that the individual with PTSD is tormented by the industrious responses of the amygdala to the past message.

Traumatic recuperation includes, to some degree, turning the hippocampus and the slower data preparing course on indeed. When that is cultivated, the cortex, with the guide of the hippocampus, will be ready to perceive that the injury is never again happening and thus will advise the amygdala to stop its steady alert. An effective result will, for the most part, observe the physical side effects that have been brought about by the amygdala's consistent caution (e.g., palpitations, focus troubles, anxiety) die down.

Central Nervous System

The central sensory system is the control community for all body and mind frameworks. The term is utilized conversely to allude to both the body's whole sensory system and furthermore to the focal piece of the sensory system, the cerebrum, and the spinal line. The nerves that radiate from the spinal string are separated into two significant orders, those that direct the engine sensory system and the ones associated with the tactile sensory system.

Tactile Nervous System

The engine sensory system (see the following area) typically gets the most consideration in books and preparing on injury and PTSD, especially the autonomic sensory system. Nonetheless; the tactile sensory system holds numerous keys for seeing how the limbic framework, especially the amygdala, reacts to injury. Too, working straightforwardly with the tangible sensory system can help numerous injury survivors to recover their balance solidly into the security of the present time and place.

There are two classifications of tangible nerves: exteroceptive and interoceptive. The exteroceptors are nerves of the five detects: locate, hearing, taste, contact, and smell. These are the faculties that assemble data from nature outer to our bodies. The other class the interoceptors, get a contribution from our inside condition: balance, interior sensations, and the capacity to find all pieces of our body without looking (proprioception).

Focusing on the tactile sensory system can be critical when attempting to resolve injury. It is the data from the faculties that the amygdala uses to decide if a condition is protected or hazardous and how to react (grin, run, etc).

A typical propensity for the individuals who experience the ill effects of PTSD, just as frenzy and nervousness issues, is their inclination to put a lopsided measure of accentuation on their interoceptive sensations. This is reasonable from the angle that those conditions hold on for them exceptionally awkward physical sensations (e.g., fast pulse, wooziness). Be that as it may, issues emerge when the individual uses those five discomforting interior sensations to pass judgment on the wellbeing or threat of the outer condition. In these occurrences, people neglect to utilize their exteroceptors, their faculties of sight, hearing, smell, etc, to really assess a present circumstance. They might be so overpowered by heart palpitations, for model, that they expect what is happening is perilous without really knowing whether that is the situation. This can form into a sort of trap, survivors accepting that either circumstance is perilous on the grounds that of what they are feeling within. It is a tricky procedure. As a general rule, one is most secure when ready to utilize exteroceptors to assess a circumstance or condition, however, for some injury survivors, this is a troublesome idea to get a handle on and a provoking procedure to instruct. The exit from this quandary is to build up double mindfulness that will make conceivable focusing on both interior and outside faculties all the while.

Engine Nervous System

All muscles are a piece of the engine's sensory system. There are two divisions, the physical and the autonomic. Muscles of the substantial sensory system are the skeletal muscles, every one of which comes to over a joint. Development is made conceivable through the compression and unwinding of the muscles that move the bones on either side of the joint either closer to or progressively far off from one another. For model, to bite a bit of gum, the jaw muscles must substitute constriction and unwinding. This makes development conceivable between the upper and lower jawbones by thus bringing them closer together and afterward more distant separated once more. Any muscle that encourages an activity (strolling, composing) or forestalls an activity (keeps down a drive) is a piece of the physical sensory system.

The autonomic sensory system contains the viscera and instinctive muscles, for example, the heart, lungs, and digestion tracts. While most activity in the physical sensory system can be cognizant or willful, the autonomic sensory system works consequently. Truth be told, it is once in a while called the programmed apprehensive framework as more often than not it is working outside of our mindfulness. Both the autonomic and physical sensory systems are engaged with reaction to injury. When defied with risk, the amygdala will guide the autonomic sensory system to stir the body to guarded activity. It does this through the hormones of adrenaline and noradrenaline, which increment pulse and breath to send heaps of oxygen to the muscles (physical sensory system). This makes conceivable either solid and brisk development for flight or fight, or loss of motion of the muscles (either firm or slack) for the defensive freeze reaction. When not in a condition of pressure, the amygdala will coordinate the autonomic sensory system to slow down body reactions, easing back heart and breath and coordinating bloodstream to the viscera to help absorption and disposal. In that state, muscles are progressively loose (as restricted to slack) and rest and rebuilding are conceivable.

Cortisol

Cortisol is closely linked with stress. It is a hormone that works as a key player in the body's stress response and is often measured in research as an indicator of stress. Cortisol plays a vital role in the body's functioning; it's secreted by the adrenal glands and involved in the following functions and more: Proper glucose metabolism, regulation of blood pressure, insulin release for blood sugar maintenance, Immune function, Inflammatory response

Cortisol: Everything You Need to Know About the 'Stress Hormone'

In some cases it is called "the pressure hormone," cortisol assumes a job in numerous illnesses and conditions. The hormone cortisol assumes a significant job in the body's pressure reaction. Cortisol is a steroid hormone that causes the body reacts to pressure. It's occasionally called the "stress hormone." That's since levels of cortisol in the body spike during times of high pressure. Steroid hormones are a class of hormones incorporated normally in the body from cholesterol. Aggregately, they complete a wide scope of capacities in the body.

Cortisol and Metabolism: What to Know
Cortisol, explicitly, assumes job indigestion. It invigorates the liver to build a generation of glucose. It likewise enables the body to change over fats, proteins, and sugars into usable vitality. As a component of the body's fight-or-flight reaction, cortisol is discharged during upsetting occasions to give your body a characteristic jolt of energy. This lift is intended to fuel your muscles to react to a compromising circumstance. Be that as it may, when cortisol levels are continually high, because of constant pressure, these equivalent impacts may bring about insulin obstruction and type 2 diabetes. Cortisol likewise enables the body to fight irritation, control the parity of salt and water in the body, and direct circulatory strain.

This hormone is delivered by the adrenal organs, two little, triangular-formed organs that sit one over every kidney. From the adrenal organs, cortisol can be discharged legitimately into the circulatory system.

The pituitary organ (a pea-sized organ at the base of the mind) and nerve center (a district of the cerebrum that controls the movement of the pituitary organ) can detect whether the blood has the perfect measure of cortisol in it.

These two cerebrum areas cooperate to guide the adrenal organs to deliver pretty much cortisol, fundamentally going about as the control component with respect to how a lot of cortisol is made. This association between the nerve center, pituitary organ, and adrenal organs shapes the foundation of the body's pressure reaction framework.

Cortisol Levels: What Do They Mean?

Levels of the hormone cortisol rise and fall normally for the duration of the day. Cortisol levels arrive at their most minimal levels late around evening time — typically around midnight From that point, levels start to rise. Cortisol arrives at its most elevated level in the body promptly in the first part of the day, cresting around 9 a.m., before starting to decrease again all through the later day. The example can change or get adjusted if individuals work sporadic moves or rest a great deal during the day. Maladies, including adrenal organ issue, that influence the generation or utilization of cortisol additionally can upset the typical example. Adrenal organ issues may emerge when the adrenal organs produce excessively or too little cortisol.

In Cushing's disorder, there's a lot of cortisol creation, while adrenal inadequacy (AI) is set apart by too little cortisol generation.

Cushing's Syndrome and Cortisol: What to Know

Cushing's disorder happens when there is a lot of cortisol in the blood for a drawn-out timeframe. This can cause physical and mental changes.

Cushing's disorder side effects may include:

- Weight gain
- High pulse
- High glucose
- Muscle misfortune and shortcoming
- Swelling of the face
- Depression
- Skin that wounds effectively
- Problems thinking plainly

The most widely recognized reason for Cushing's disorder is taking steroid-type drugs, for example, prednisone, which is basically fundamentally the same as cortisol. This sort of Cushing's disorder normally leaves after the drug is halted.

Cushing's disorder additionally can be brought about by a little tumor on the pituitary organ.

Adrenal Insufficiency and Cortisol: What to Know
Adrenal inadequacy happens when the adrenal organs don't make enough cortisol. This can happen when the adrenal organs don't work appropriately (Addison's infection) or when the pituitary organ doesn't immediate the adrenal organs to make cortisol.

Manifestations of adrenal inadequacy can include:

- Severe exhaustion and shortcoming

- Weight misfortune

- Faintness or unsteadiness, particularly after standing

- Low circulatory strain

- Low glucose

- Darkened skin on the face, neck, and back of hands

Individuals with an adrenal deficiency may need to take a sort of steroid hormone drug, called glucocorticoids, to raise their cortisol levels.

Testing Cortisol Levels
Your social insurance supplier may suggest having your cortisol levels tried in the event that the individual in question speculates you may have nearly nothing or an excessive amount of cortisol generation.

Cortisol levels can be estimated in blood, pee, or salivation. Blood tests might be taken from a vein in the arm in the first part of the day when levels are most elevated. Tests may likewise be taken around 4 pm toward the evening when levels ought to be significantly lower. The blood test for low cortisol is finished by estimating levels in the blood both previously and an hour after the infusion of a medication called adrenocorticotropic hormone (ACTH). ACTH is a pituitary organ hormone that animates cortisol generation. In patients with a low cortisol level brought about by Addison's disease, the levels won't rise significantly after infusion of ACTH, though in typical people the levels rise impressively. Spit additionally might be gathered. During a salivation cortisol test, you will be approached to embed a swab into your mouth and hold up a couple of moments until it is soaked with spit.

For a cortisol pee test, you might be approached to gather all the pee you produce over a 24-hour time span in a holder given by the research facility. In any case, urinary cortisol levels can once in a while be tried with a solitary example of the principal pee toward the beginning of the day.

Adrenal Fatigue and Cortisol
The expression "adrenal weakness" as of late has been utilized in the media — and by some medicinal services experts — to portray a large group of ambiguous manifestations, including tiredness, body throbs, apprehension, and rest and stomach related issues. The general thought is that steady pressure may cause the cortisol-delivering adrenal organs to "wear out" and quit creating their significant hormones.

There's no logical proof that adrenal weakness exists. The possibility that pressure makes the adrenal organs "wear out" and quit making cortisol isn't predictable with logical comprehension of how the adrenal organs work. Stress really expands cortisol creation.

Neither the Endocrine Society — the world's biggest association of hormone issue specialists — nor some other significant medicinal association perceives adrenal weariness as an authentic therapeutic analysis.

Cortisol, Metabolism, and Weight Gain

There's been a great deal of research connecting incessant worry to weight increase and stoutness in ongoing decades. Cortisol — discharged from the adrenal organs into the circulation system during unpleasant circumstances — assumes significant job indigestion, driving specialists to speculate that always elevated levels of cortisol may assume a job in weight gain.

Some creature thinks about have indicated that an excessive amount of cortisol can advance the amassing of midsection fat. What's more, specialists realize that people and lab creatures will, in general, decide on vitality thick nourishments when under consistent pressure, driving some to propose that constantly high cortisol levels additionally may assume a job in causing us to long for unhealthy solace food sources.

Be that as it may, logical examinations in people have turned up blended outcomes on the connection between high cortisol and weight gain, with certain investigations finding a connection and others not. An extensive survey of logical and restorative investigations, distributed in October 2012 in the diary Obesity, found no reliable connection between cortisol levels and paunch fat.

A large number of these more seasoned investigations estimated cortisol levels in blood, pee, or salivation. While these natural liquids can fill in as great markers for day by day changes in cortisol levels and help specialists evaluate when to an extreme or too little cortisol is being delivered, a few researchers have contended that they may not give the most precise image of extended cortisol introduction.

In a huge investigation of in excess of 2,500 British grown-ups, analysts estimated cortisol focuses in hair. They found that individuals with higher hair cortisol levels over a multi-year time frame were bound to be fat — and to remain fat — than individuals with lower levels. The scientists, who distributed their examination in February 2017 in the diary Obesity, said that hair cortisol might be a superior marker of extended cortisol introduction — and constant pressure — than cortisol levels estimated in blood, pee, or salivation.

Positive Effects

During the day, the cortisol level in various individuals can fluctuate, this can happen even to the Same People. Taking an instance, the level of cortisol is more during the day than nights, and this discovery is in a repeated cycle. Fluctuations can be as a result of what an individual is currently experiencing at that time. For example, in spite of the fact that pressure isn't the main reason why cortisol is emitted into the circulatory system, it has been named "the stress hormone" since it's level of discharge is high when the body responds to stress, and it's also the reason behind various stress based changes in the body. Little increments of cortisol have some beneficial outcomes: Elevated memory processes, increase in immunity, and balance of body homeostasis.

A few people experience a more prominent spike in cortisol than others when they experience pressure. in response to stressors, it is additionally conceivable to limit the measure of cortisol you discharge. The use of pressure management techniques regularly, can be employed to achieve this result. An in-depth discussion would be done later in this book.

Effects of Too Much Cortisol and Stress

While cortisol is a significant and accommodating piece of the body's reaction to stretch, it's significant that the body's unwinding reaction be enacted so the body's capacities can come back to typical after a distressing occasion. Tragically, in our present high-stress culture, the body's pressure reaction is enacted so regularly that the body doesn't generally get an opportunity to come back to typical, bringing about a condition of incessant pressure. Higher and progressively drawn out degrees of cortisol in the circulatory system, (for example, those related with interminable pressure) have been appeared to have negative impacts, for example, Weakened psychological execution, stifled thyroid capacity, Blood sugar uneven characters for example, hyperglycemia, Decreased bone thickness, Decrease in muscle tissue, higher blood pressure. Brought down insusceptibility and fiery reactions in the body, eased back injury recuperating, and other wellbeing outcomes. Expanded stomach fat, which is related to a more noteworthy measure of medical issues than fat stored in different territories of the body.. Some of the health problems associated with increased stomach fat are heart attacks, strokes, developing metabolic syndrome, higher levels of "bad" cholesterol (LDL) and lower levels of "good" cholesterol (HDL), which can lead to other health problems.

Cortisol and You

As mentioned before, cortisol secretion varies among individuals. People are biologically 'wired' to react differently to stress. One person may secrete higher levels of cortisol than another in the same situation. And this tendency can change at different times in a person's life. Studies have also shown that people who secrete higher levels of cortisol in response to stress also tend to eat more food and food that is higher in carbohydrates than people who secrete less cortisol. If you're more sensitive to stress, it's especially important for you to learn stress management techniques and maintain a low-stress lifestyle. this is a great way to get cortisol secretion under control and maintain a healthy lifestyle at the same time.

You will be getting more information on stress and resources to help you to manage it can help you to build habits that can help you to cope with stress once your stress response is triggered.

The Role of Cortisol

In the previous scarcely any years, the job of cortisol in light of and recuperation from injury has become befuddled. Since it is a piece of the whole situation of reaction to injury, to be sure a pressure hormone, cortisol has gotten wrongly viewed by numerous individuals as something that builds pressure. This is really not the case and a basic looking over of cortisol examine, especially that by Rachel Yehuda and six other partners (1990, 1995), who originally found the job of cortisol in injury, explains the issue. With respect to the injury reaction, cortisol is an indispensable companion. The discourse of the amygdala and hippocampus concentrated on what happens to lay the foundation for the improvement of PTSD. The picture is very unique in the situation that leads the other way, to goals.

At the point when a horrible circumstance has finished and the individual has made due through flight or fight, the amygdala guides the adrenal organs to discharge cortisol to hose the injury reaction. Cortisol ends the excitement and helps the autonomic sensory system to swing from a condition of worry to a condition of quiet. Actually, one of the challenges for individuals with PTSD is that their cortisol levels are lower than expected.

Cortisol has not had the option to carry out its responsibility for them. In years past, endeavors were made to infuse those with PTSD with cortisol with the expectation that it is ready to do likewise afterward. Be that as it may, none of these examinations indicated a lot of guarantee for a postponed presentation of cortisol. For those intrigued by the job of cortisol in different conditions, look especially to contemplates melancholy.

Apparently, those experiencing sorrow normally have raised degrees of cortisol. On the off chance that conclusion is in question, basically surveying cortisol levels will highlight an individual's more prominent propensity toward gloom or on the other hand PTSD.

How to Stay Balanced

To keep cortisol levels healthy and under control, the body's relaxation response should be activated after the fight or flight response occurs. You can learn to relax your body with various stress management techniques, and you can make lifestyle changes in order to keep your body from reacting to stress in the first place. The following have been found by many to be very helpful in relaxing the body and mind, aiding the body in maintaining healthy cortisol levels:

Guided Imagery

Journaling

Self-Hypnosis

Exercise

Yoga

Listening to Music

Breathing Exercises

Meditation

Sex

Chapter 4 SAFE WAYS TO PRACTICE POLYVAGAL THEORY

Yoga

10 Yoga Poses You Need to Know

The structure squares of yoga are presents. These are acceptable ones to learn as you construct a standard yoga practice.

These 10 stances are a finished yoga exercise. Move gradually through each posture, making sure to inhale as you move. Delay after any posture you find testing, particularly in the event that you are shy of breath, and start again when your breathing normalizes+. The thought is to hold each model for a couple, slow breaths before proceeding onward to the following one.

Child's Pose

This quieting present is a decent default delay position. You can utilize the kid's posture to rest and pull together before proceeding to your next posture. It tenderly stretches your lower back, hips, thighs, knees and lower legs and loosens up your spine, shoulders and neck.

Do it: When you need to get a decent delicate stretch through your neck spine and hips.

Skip it: If you have knee wounds or lower leg issues. Maintain a strategic distance from likewise on the off chance that you have hypertension or are pregnant.

Change: You can lay your head on a pad or square. You can put a moved towel under your lower legs on the off chance that they are awkward.

Be careful: Focus on loosening up the muscles of the spine and lower back as you relax.

This ought to be your go-to present at whatever point you have to rest for a minute during a yoga exercise.

The child's posture extends your back muscles, hips, thighs, and lower legs. Legitimate act of this asana can help mitigate spinal pain. This posture loosens up the body and encourages you to rest better.

Attempt IT!

Steps

Bow down on the yoga tangle.

Move into a situated position gradually, by laying your hips on your heels.

Twist forward to lay your brow on the tangle.

Keep your hands straight – stretch them before you. You will feel the back muscles stretch a bit.

Move the legs separated to keep the chest open, your midsection ought to be between the two legs.

Remain in the stance for in any event three to four breaths.

To discharge – gradually pull your upper-middle up and get your hands on your sides.

This is one of the most widely recognized yoga presents. Posing as a downward-facing dog assuages stress, extends the hamstrings and calves, fortifies hands and legs, and empowers the body.

Attempt IT!

<u>Steps</u>.

Set yourself for the posture with your hands and knees on the floor. Your knees ought to be opposite to your hips, while your hands ought to be under the shoulders.

Spread your palms and gradually move your hands somewhat forward, while squeezing the fingers on the tangle for grasp.

Turn or twist your toes under and gradually drive the hips up, to make a rearranged V with your body. Your knees ought not to be contacting the ground now.

Ensure your feet are hip-width separated and the knees are marginally twisted.

Remain in the situation for three breath cycles.

To discharge, twist the knees gradually and move over into the underlying situation, with your hands under the shoulder and the knees under the hip.

Plank Pose

A normally observed exercise, board helps manufacture quality in the center, shoulders, arms, and legs. This normal posture can construct quality in the center, shoulders, arms, and legs.

Do it: Plank present is acceptable in the event that you are hoping to condition your abs and fabricate quality in your chest area.

Skip it: Avoid board present in the event that you experience the ill effects of carpal passage disorder. It tends to be no picnic for your wrists. You may likewise skip it or adjust on the off chance that you have low back agony.

Change: You can alter it by setting your knees on the floor.

Be careful: As you do aboard, envision the rear of your neck and spine stretching.

Attempt IT!

Try not to rehearse the full form of the posture on the off chance that you have carpal passage disorder — either practice the posture on your knees in Half Plank Pose or on your lower arms. Those with osteoporosis ought to likewise keep away from Plank Pose because of the danger of breaks. Continuously work inside your own scope of points of confinement and capacities. On the off chance that you have any medical concerns, converse with your PCP before rehearsing yoga.

Steps

Start on your hands and knees, with your wrists straightforwardly under your shoulders. Inhale easily and equitably through your nose. Expedite your contemplations to center the present minute.

Spread your fingers and press down through your lower arms and hands. Try not to allow your chest to fall.

Look down between your hands, protracting the rear of your neck and drawing your stomach muscles toward your spine.

Fold your toes and venture back with your feet, bringing your body and head into one straight line.

Keep your thighs lifted and take care not to let your hips sink excessively low. In the event that your butt stands undetermined, realign your body so your shoulders are straightforwardly over your wrists.

Draw your pelvic floor muscles toward your spine as you contract your stomach muscles. Keep your head in accordance with your spine. Expand over your shoulder bones and over your collarbones.

Drawdown through the bases of your forefingers — don't let your hands move open toward the pinkie fingers.

Step 8

Press the front of your thighs (quadriceps) up toward the roof while stretching your tailbone toward your heels.

Step 5

Hold the posture while breathing easily for five breaths. On the off chance that you are utilizing the posture to fabricate quality and stamina, hold for as long as five minutes. To discharge, gradually lower onto your knees, at that point press once more into Child's Pose and rest. Those rehearsing Sun Salutations should move straightforwardly from Plank into Chaturanga or Knees-

Chest-Chin Pose.

Changes and Variations

Plank Pose can be a brilliant center and arm strengthener when drilled accurately. It can require some investment to develop enough solidarity to hold the posture for in excess of a breath or two. Take it gradually and be mindful so as not to over-stress your arms and shoulders. To extend or help the posture, attempt these basic changes to discover the variety that works best for you:

On the off chance that your arms or abs are not yet sufficiently able to help your full body weight, you can bring down your knees to the floor (this is called Half Plank Pose). Make certain to keep your head and spine in a straight line. To extend the posture, have a go at lifting each leg in turn. Hold the lifted leg for five breaths. At that point, rehash with the contrary leg for a similar measure of time.

In the event that your wrists get sore, roll the top edge of your tangle a couple of times. Spot the base of the palms of your hands on the moving segment of the tangle, with your fingers delicately twisting. Press down through the base of your pointers.

Board Pose can construct a great deal of solidarity and stamina all through the body when it's finished with the right arrangement. Remember the accompanying data while rehearsing it:

Try not to enable your hips and butt to list excessively low or jab excessively high — it's imperative to keep your body in one straight line, from shoulders to heels.

Keep your shoulders adjusted straightforwardly over your wrists.

The separation between your hands and feet ought to be the equivalent in both Plank Pose and Downward-Facing Dog. Move to and fro between the two to figure out the right separation.

Keep the space between your shoulder bones wide while expanding over your neckline bones. This activity sets you up for more profound arm adjusts, similar to Crow Pose.

Never lock your elbows in the posture — doing so can prompt hyperextension and damage. Rather, keep them delicate by connecting with your biceps and triceps, making a "small scale twist" in the joint.

Rehearsing Plank Pose will fortify your center and arms in a matter of moments. Holding it for expanded periods will assemble continuance and assurance. Discover a variety or alteration that works best for you, and afterward watch as your capacity increments!

This push-up variety follows board present in a typical yoga grouping known as the sun greeting. It is a decent posture to learn on the off chance that you need to in the long run work on further developed stances, for example, arm adjusts or reversals.

Do it: Like the board, this posture fortifies arms and wrists and tones the stomach area.

Skip it: If you have carpal passage disorder, lower back torment, shoulder damage or are pregnant.

Adjust: It's a smart thought for amateurs to alter the posture by keeping your knees on the floor.

Be careful: Press your palms equitably into the floor and lift your shoulders from the floor as you hold this posture.

Four-Limbed Staff Pose or (Chaturanga Dandasana)

This posture fabricates quality in the arms, shoulders, wrists, and back and helps tone the belly.

Attempt IT!

Step 1

Perform Downward Dog pose, at that point Plank Pose. Firm your shoulder bones against your back ribs and press your tailbone toward your pubis.

Step 2

With an exhalation gradually bring down your middle and legs to a couple of creeps above and parallel to the floor.

There's a propensity in this posture for the lower back to influence toward the floor and the tailbone to jab up toward the roof. All through your stay in this position, keep the tailbone solidly set up and the legs dynamic and turned somewhat internal. Draw the pubis toward the navel.

Stage 3

Keep the space between the shoulder bones wide. Try not to let the elbows spread out to the sides; hold them in by the sides of the middle and drive them back toward the heels. Press the bases of the forefingers immovably to the floor. Lift the highest point of the sternum and your head to look forward.

Stage 4

Four-Limbed Staff Pose is one of the situations in the Sun Salutation grouping. You can likewise rehearse this posture separately for somewhere in the range of 10 to 30 seconds. Discharge with an exhalation. Either lay yourself delicately down onto the floor or push emphatically back to Downward Dog pose, lifting through the top thighs and the tailbone.

Cobra Pose

This back-twisting posture can help reinforce the back muscles, increment spinal adaptability and stretches the chest, shoulders, and guts.

Do it: This post is extraordinary for reinforcing the back.

Skip it: If you have joint inflammation in your spine or neck, a low-back damage or carpal passage disorder.

Adjust: Just lift up a couple of inches, and don't attempt to fix your arms.

Be careful: Try to keep your navel drawing up away from the floor as you hold this posture.

Cobra Pose

One of the less difficult back-twisting stances.

Attempt IT!

Stage 1

Untruth inclined on the floor. Stretch your legs back, highest points of the feet on the floor. Spread your hands on the floor under your shoulders. Embrace the elbows again into your body.

See additionally Using Cobra Pose for Safe Stretching

Stage 2

Press the highest points of the feet and thighs and the pubis immovably into the floor.

See additionally More Back Bend Poses

Stage 3

On an inward breath, start to fix the arms to lift the chest off the floor, going just to the stature at which you can keep up an association through your pubis to your legs. Press the tailbone toward the pubis and lift the pubis toward the navel. Thin the hip focuses. Firm, however, don't solidify the rear end.

Stage 4

Firm the shoulder bones against the back, puffing the side ribs forward. Lift through the highest point of the sternum however abstain from driving the front ribs forward, which just solidifies the lower back. Appropriate the backbend equitably all through the whole spine.

Stage 5

Hold the posture somewhere in the range of 15 to 30 seconds, breathing effectively. Discharge back to the floor with an exhalation.

Tree Pose

Past improving your equalization, it can likewise reinforce your center, lower legs, calves, thighs, and spine.

Do it: Great for chipping away at your parity and stance.

Skip it: You may need to skirt this posture on the off chance that you have low circulatory strain or any ailments that influence your parity.

Adjust: Place one of your hands on a divider for help.

Be careful: Focus on your breath in and out as you hold this posture.

Tree Pose

This adjusting present is one of the most perceived postures in current yoga.

Attempt IT!

Steps 1

Remain with your feet together, inward lower legs and

internal knees contacting. Locate a straight line of vitality through the focal point of the body, from the internal curves up through the crown of the head. Unite the hands at the focal point of the chest in Anjali Mudra. Breathe out, root down through your feet, and feel dauntlessness, immovability, and establishing in Tadasana, or Mountain Pose.

Steps 2

Move your weight onto your correct foot. Twist your left knee, and push it toward the chest. Keeping along the spine, reach down and fasten your left lower leg. Spot the bottom of the left foot on the internal right thigh.

Steps 3

Extend your tailbone toward the floor to stand tall and bring your Drishti, or look, to the divider straightforwardly before you to enable you to adjust.

Steps 4

Press your left foot into the internal right thigh and your correct thigh into your foot with an end goal to keep up your midline.

Steps 5

Square the two hips to the front of the room, keeping your forgot about knee moving to one side.

Steps 6

Firm your external right thigh by getting the quadriceps muscles, or the front of the thighs. Zip your tummy in and your lower ribs together. Lift the chest and cut the shoulder bones down.

Steps 7

Take 5–10 full breaths, discovering length on each breathes in and establishing down with each breathes out.

Steps 8

Breathe out and discharge the left leg back to Tadasana. Rehash on the opposite side.

Triangle Pose

Triangle, which is a piece of numerous yoga successions helps assemble quality in the legs and stretches the hips, spine, chest, shoulders, crotches, hamstrings and calves. It can likewise help increment versatility in the hips and neck.

Do it: This posture is incredible for building quality and continuance.

Skip it: Avoid this posture in the event that you have a cerebral pain or low circulatory strain.

Alter: If you have hypertension, turn your head to look descending in the last posture. On the off chance that you have neck issues, don't turn your head to look upward; look straight ahead and keep the two sides of the neck long.

Be careful: Keep lifting your raised arm toward the roof. It helps keep the posture light.

Triangle Pose

This posture can be found in numerous yoga successions.

Attempt IT

Step 1

From a standing situation with the legs 3 feet separated as in Five Pointed Star, turn the correct toes to the correct divider and the left toes marginally inwards. Breathe in and press the forgot about hips to one side as you slide the two arms to the correct parallel to the floor.

Step 2

Breathe out and pivot just the arms, raising the left arm up and resting the correct hand against the correct leg, with the palms looking ahead.

Step 3

Press into the feet, pull up the knee tops, keeping the legs solid. Arrive at the fingertips from one another, bringing the arms into one straight line with the shoulders stacked over one another. Press the left hip forward and the correct hip back.

Step 4

Inhale and hold for 3-6 breaths.

Step 5

To discharge: breathe in and arrive at the lifted hand up towards the roof as you push down into the feet utilizing the entire body to lift once again into 5 pointed star.

Step 6

Rehash on the opposite side.

Advantages: Triangle present connects all aspects of the body, reinforces the center, opens the hips and shoulders and stretches the legs.

Contraindications: Recent or interminable damage to the hips, back or bears.

Situated Half-Spinal Twist Pose

This contorting posture can build the adaptability in your back while extending the shoulders, hips, and chest. It can likewise help soothe strain in your back.

Do it: To discharge tight muscles around the shoulders and upper and lower back.

Skip it: If you have back damage.

Alter: If twisting your correct knee is awkward, keep it straight out before you.

Be careful: Lift your middle with each breathes in, and contort as you breathe out.

Situated Half Spinal Twist Pose Need to ease the pressure in your back? Attempt this bending present.

Attempt IT!

After the forward and in reverse bowing of the spine, the Half Spinal Twist gives a parallel stretch which calms general lower back torment and solid ailment of the back and hips. Every vertebra is turned in the two headings. The

Half Spinal Twist has numerous gainful consequences for the nerve bladder, spleen, kidneys, liver, and digestion tracts. The muscular strength is kneaded and the digestive organ specifically is invigorated. This soothes blockage, acid reflux, and other stomach related problems. On the otherworldly level, this posture is likewise known to help raise kuṇḍalinī.

Objective: To keep up sideways versatility in your spine.

Stage 1 – Legs Bent

Sit up on your heels. Drop your posterior to the floor, to one side of your legs.

Stage 2 – Leg Position

Curve your correct leg. Traverse your left leg, and spot it on the floor by the outside of your left knee. Keeping your arm straight, put your correct hand level on the floor despite your good faith. Arms: Lay your correct hand on the floor. Raise your left arm straight up.

Stage 3 – The Twist

Lower your left arm, bringing it outside your twisted knee, at that point handle your correct lower leg. Hold for at any rate 30 seconds. Rehash, bending the other way.

Bridge Pose

This is a back-twisting represent that stretches the muscles of the chest, back, and neck. It likewise fabricates quality in the back and hamstring muscles.

Do it: If you sit the vast majority of the day, this posture will assist you with opening your upper chest.

Skip it: Avoid this posture on the off chance that you have neck damage.

Alter: Place a square between your thighs to help keep the legs and feet in a legitimate arrangement. Or then again you can put a square under your pelvis if your lower back is annoying you.

Be careful: While holding this posture, attempt to keep your chest lifted and your sternum toward your jawline.

Bridge Pose

This posture, from the back-twisting group of yoga presents, is extraordinary for extending the muscles of the chest.

Attempt IT!

Step 1

Lying on your back, twist the two knees and spot the feet level on the floor hip-width separated. Slide the arms close by the body with the palms looking down. The fingertips ought to be delicately contacting the heels.

Step 2

Press the feet into the floor, breathe in and lift the hips, rolling the spine off the floor. Softly press the knees together to keep the knees hip-width separated.

Step 3

Press down into the arms and shoulders to lift the chest up. Draw in the legs, backside and Mula bandha to lift the hips higher.

Step 4

Inhale and hold for 4-8 breaths.

Step 5

To discharge: breath out and gradually roll the spine back to the floor.

Advantages: Bridge present forms center and lower body quality, protracts and fortifies the spine, invigorates the body, and animates the endocrine and sensory systems.

Contraindications: Recent or ceaseless damage to the knees, bears or back.

Carcass Pose

Like life, yoga classes commonly end with this posture. It takes into consideration a snapshot of unwinding, yet a few people think that its hard to remain still in this posture. Be that as it may, the more you attempt this represent, the simpler it is to sink into an unwinding, sympathetic state.

Do it: Always!

Skip it: If you would prefer not to have a minute's tranquility.

Change: Place a cover under your head, if that feels progressively good. You can likewise move up a cover and spot that under your knees if your lower back is delicate or annoying you.

Be careful: Feel the heaviness of your body sinking into your tangle each part in turn.

Carcass Pose

Despite the fact that it may not look troublesome, it very well may be very testing to lie in carcass present for an all-inclusive timeframe.

Attempt IT!

Step 1

Lying on your back, let the arms and legs drop open, with the arms around 45 degrees from the side of your body. Ensure you are warm and agreeable, on the off chance that you have to put covers under or over your body.

Step 2

Close the eyes, and take moderate full breaths through the nose. Enable your entire body to turn out to be delicate and overwhelming, letting it unwind into the floor. As the body unwinds, feel the entire body rising and falling with every breath.

Step 3

Output the body from the toes to the fingers to the crown of the head, searching for pressure, snugness and contracted muscles. Intentionally discharge and loosen up any regions that you find. On the off chance that you have to, rock or squirm portions of your body from side to side to empower further discharge.

Step 4

Discharge all control of the breath, the psyche, and the body. Let your body move further and more profound into a condition of all-out unwinding.

Step 5

Remain in corpse pose for 5 to 15 minutes.

Step 6

To discharge: gradually develop the breath, squirm the fingers and toes, arrive at the arms over your head and stretch the entire body, breathe out twist the knees into the chest and turn over to the other side coming into a fetal position. At the point when you are prepared, gradually breathe in up to a situated position.

Advantages: Corpse present is fundamental to rehearse toward the finish of each yoga practice. This stance revives the body, psyche and soul while diminishing pressure and strain.

Contraindications: Third trimester of pregnancy.

The last posture of any yoga class is one of profound rebuilding: Corpse Pose, likewise now and then called Final Relaxation Pose. Its Sanskrit name, "Corpse Pose" (shah-VAHS-uh-nuh), originates from two words. The first is "Sava" (signifying "carcass"), and the second is "asana" (signifying "present"). Corpse pose infers a profundity of discharge that goes past straightforward unwinding. This resting present takes your yoga practice to a spot where you can totally give up.

In spite of the fact that it might appear to be a simple posture, Corpse pose can really be exceptionally hard to learn and rehearse well. The extraordinary yoga experts K. Pattabhi Jois and B.K.S. Iyengar even called Corpse to pose the most troublesome of all yoga presents. For some understudies, the capacity to lie totally still — like a body — while being both completely mindful of and unattached from the present minute takes a lot of training and tolerance. In contrast to dynamic, moving, and physically requesting postures, Corpse pose requires a cognizant choice to discharge the psychological babble and give up completely into a condition of essence.

The Most Important Pose in Yoga

Many, if not most, yoga customs and yoga instructors see Corpse pose as the absolute most significant posture of your training. For a certain something, it permits your body time to process the data and advantages got from the stances ("asanas") and breathing activities ("pranayama"). Yet, the advantages of Corpse pose are substantially more than simply physical — this posture upgrades and reestablishes the body, brain, and soul.

Corpse pose isn't rest time — you don't really nod off when rehearsing it. Rather, the thought is to stay present and mindful for the total term of the posture. Doing so enables the psychological prattle to settle, bringing your mindfulness much more profound into your deepest and most elevated condition of cognizance. As you go further, you can start to discharge the tangled bunches of examples ("samskaras"), feelings, and thoughts that unwittingly control your life — liberating you to turn out to be all the more entire and complete in your actual quintessence.

Through the way toward rehearsing Corpse pose, you can start to see your existence with greater clearness and new mindfulness. The reviving and mind-clearing parts of Corpse pose give you the devices to manage pressure and feelings throughout your life off the tangle.

Advantages of Corpse pose

In spite of the fact that it's occasionally used to start practice, Corpse pose is frequently used to end practice to permit your body, psyche, and soul to completely unwind and discharge strain. It's an opportunity to let waiting considerations and stresses blur away. From the profundity and dimness of Corpse pose, you can be restored, invigorated, and renewed.

The profoundly loosening up part of Corpse pose is known to be remedial for stress. At the point when you're under pressure, your sympathetic sensory system delivers a "fight or flight" reaction that can over-animate your brain and body, causing nervousness, weariness, sadness, and disease. On the other hand, rehearsing Corpse pose invigorates the parasympathetic sensory system — known as the "rest and condensation" reaction. Loosening up the physical body in Corpse pose has various advantages, including: Brought down circulatory strain, A diminished pulse, Eased back pace of breath, Diminished muscle strain, Diminished metabolic rate, The physical reaction can additionally result in Diminished event of migraines, Help from weakness and sleep deprivation, Diminished apprehensive strain, Help from uneasiness and fits of anxiety, Expanded in general vitality levels, Expanded efficiency, Improved focus and memory, Clearheadedness and a feeling of core interest, Increased self-assurance.

Notwithstanding the mind-body benefits, Corpse pose is likewise a period during your training when you can associate with your serene, deepest self. "Yoga" is frequently interpreted as "association," alluding to the association between your brain, body, and soul. At the point when you subside into Corpse pose and become mindful of this association, you are genuinely rehearsing yoga.

Corpse pose is the place individuals are destined to encounter the importance of yoga, which is their cognizant solidarity with Infinity… You lie there and look dead, however as you unwind and sink into the sentiment of the alive vitality that is being you, it truly feels like you spring up once more.

Caution

Corpse pose is suitable for all yoga understudies. In the event that you are awkward lying on your back, practice a bolstered rendition of the posture (see Modifications and

116

Variations, underneath). Ladies who are pregnant should keep their head and chest brought up in the posture by laying on support or pad. Continuously work inside your very own scope of breaking points and capacities. In the event that you have any restorative concerns, converse with your primary care physician before rehearsing yoga.

Guidelines

- Lie on your back with your legs straight and arms at your sides. Rest your hands around six inches from your body with your palms up. Let your feet drop open. Close your eyes. You might need to cover your body with a cover.

- Let your breath happen normally.

- Enable your body to feel overwhelming on the ground.

- Working from the bottoms of your feet up to the crown of your head, deliberately discharge each body part, organ, and cell.

- Loosen up your face. Let your eyes drop profound into their attachments. Welcome harmony and quietness into your psyche, body, and soul.

- Remain in Corpse pose for five minutes for at regular intervals of your training.

To leave the posture, initially start to develop your breath. Taking delicate development and mindfulness back to your body, squirming your fingers and toes. Move to your correct side and rest there for a minute. With an inward breath, tenderly press yourself into an agreeable situated position. Leave your head alone the exact opposite thing to come into place. Convey the harmony and stillness of Corpse pose with you all through the remainder of your day.

Changes and Variations

Since Corpse pose is such a significant posture — and is regularly polished for a few minutes — it's indispensable to feel great when rehearsing it. Make whatever changes you have to feel completely bolstered in the posture. Here are a few proposals:

The body regularly chills off essentially after training while resting in Corpse pose. You might need to keep a sweeping, sweater, or a couple of socks close by to cover yourself up before sinking into the posture.

On the off chance that your low back is tight, it very well may be hard to lie on your back serenely. Putting a reinforce underneath your knees drops weight from your pelvis, which can permit the lumbar vertebrae and lower back to discharge and unwind.

Try not to be hesitant to utilize props, regardless of whether you needn't bother with them! For example, eye pads do some incredible things to shut out the light in a studio with brilliant windows or non-dimmable lights. In the event that you don't have an eye cushion, place a collapsed towel over your eyes. You can likewise attempt a reinforce under your knees; 10-pound sand packs hung over your thighs; or a collapsed cover underneath your shoulder bones.

Ladies who are pregnant ought not to lie totally level in Corpse pose. Rather, rest the chest area on a reinforce or pile of firm cushions and covers, keeping the chest and head over the stomach.

Tips

Regardless of whether you're pristine to yoga or have been rehearsing for a long time, one tip applies to everybody: Don't skip Corpse pose!

The last unwinding segment of your training is essential. In the event that you should leave class early, let your educator know ahead of time, and take a short Corpse pose before you leave. By and large, be that as it may, plan never to pass up this posture. Take as much time as is needed leaving the profound unwinding — doing so will assist you with keeping the quiet nearness and center all through the remainder of your day.

In the event that you wind up nodding off in Corpse pose, find a way to address weariness and rest issues outside of your yoga practice. Yoga for Insomnia and Yoga for Stress Relief if napping off in Corpse pose turns into a propensity.

Unwind to Renew

Practice Corpse pose toward the finish of each asana and pranayama session. You can likewise do Corpse pose without anyone else, instead of an evening rest or mug of espresso. As you practice Corpse pose consistently, check whether you can take advantage of that profoundly loosened up condition of internal mindfulness during your customary day. Figuring out how to get to that serene, current situation with awareness in all circumstances is the way to bringing your yoga practice off the tangle and into a mind-blowing remainder.

Yoga 101

A lot of explicit activities, called presents, joined with explicit breathing methods and reflection standards are the structure squares of a yoga class. On the off chance that a posture causes torment or demonstrates excessively troublesome, some varieties and alterations can be made to support understudies. Props like squares, covers and ties — even seats — can be utilized to assist you with getting the most profit by the stances. Yoga isn't one-size-fits-all: The best yoga exercise for you will rely upon your individual needs and objectives.

The advantages of a customary yoga practice are wide-going. By and large, a total yoga exercise can help keep your back and joints solid, improve your general stance, extend and reinforce muscles and improve your parity, says Roger Cole, Ph.D., a psychobiologist and ensured Iyengar yoga instructor. Yoga likewise has "a helpful side that is profoundly unwinding and reviving," Dr. Cole says. "Unwinding is incorporated with each yoga session."

What's more, yoga's emphasis on the breath can quiet you and assist you with figuring out how to be progressively aware of your body, says Dr. Timothy McCall, the creator of "Yoga as Medicine," and that can assist you with moving no sweat. As of late, increasingly more research is showing the wide-running medical advantages of yoga. Studies show that yoga can help:

• Reduce back torment: Weekly yoga classes soothe side effects of low back agony about just as serious, normal extending sessions.

• Strengthen bones: In one little examination, yoga expert

GUIDED IMAGERY
Guided symbolism

A viable agony the board apparatus for all-out joint substitution?

Measurements

GUIDED IMAGERY is an undeniably famous agony the executive alternative inside the logical and social insurance networks as narcotic related passings keep on rising. A mental unwinding system, guided symbolism uses mental pictures of wonderful sights, smells, sounds, tastes, or substantial sensations (contact, developments, or positions) to make a positive psychological and enthusiastic express that can forestall or improve torment or different wellsprings of distress.1 (See Types of guided symbolism.) It might be utilized as a subordinate methodology to help reduce agony and uneasiness in patients who have experienced an absolute joint substitution (TJR) of the knee or hip. Actualizing guided symbolism has been appeared to diminish torment and tension levels, improving patient fulfillment scores. Although more proof is expected to help bolster their viability for postoperative torment and uneasiness, corresponding treatments, for example, guided symbolism can possibly expand self-adequacy of patients in numerous careful circumstances. Elective TJR is a difficult methodology, and intense postoperative agony after the system can be exceptional. This article investigates the potential viability of utilizing guided symbolism for patients recuperating from TJR.

The case for nonopioid options

Pharmacologic modalities during the prompt postoperative period are frequently required and might be utilized to adequately deal with a patient's torment; be that as it may, consolidating integral treatments enables the patient to assume responsibility for their agony and recuperation. Utilizing a multimodal way to deal with torment the board during the postoperative period may diminish the measure of agony experienced by the patient. A multimodal approach utilizes different analgesics, for example, narcotics, acetaminophen, gabapentin, and nonsteroidal mitigating drugs, notwithstanding nonpharmacologic modalities, for example, ice or subjective treatments (for instance, guided symbolism) to help decline pain.4 When a patient's agony is very much overseen, the person is better ready to take an interest in active recuperation, hack, take full breaths, and focus on mending and recovering freedom.

From 1999 to 2017, around 218,000 individuals passed on from overdoses related to narcotic prescriptions. Lack of torment control in careful patients can add to longer medical clinic stays, delayed utilization of narcotics while in the emergency clinic and at home, a reduction in personal satisfaction, and trouble with mobility. It was discovered that patients who detailed utilizing narcotics before medical procedures had a higher pace of narcotic utilize a half year post-operation. Patients who take higher measures of narcotics preoperatively just as postoperatively are bound to make some troublesome memories weaning off them once their postoperative torment improves. Opioid use can cause sedation and respiratory gloom, two unfriendly responses that may obstruct early ambulation and lead to poor patient outcomes. Pain prescription may likewise hamper a patient's self-efficacy.

Information from the National Health Statistics Reports shows that 41.6% of grown-ups utilized some sort of reciprocal medication in 2012. The report features the proof of reciprocal methods being utilized to oversee torment in grown-ups with musculoskeletal issues. The National Center for Complementary and Integrative Health has recorded propelling the comprehension of the impact that the brain and body have on wellbeing as a major aspect of its 2016 Strategic Plan. Guided symbolism centers around positive or lovely symbolism to enable the brain to move away from physical and mental torment, which may prompt a lessening in tension, stress, or potential pain.

By what method can guided symbolism help?

Guided symbolism is an unwinding procedure that can help decrease pressure and uneasiness as patients are guided to envision themselves healing. (See Using guided symbolism: A model.) Guided symbolism utilizes every one of the faculties to associate the psyche and body. Patients ought to be urged to imagine themselves with diminished agony and to receive an uplifting attitude toward their normal results and wellbeing handling. In a twofold visually impaired randomized examination on same-day careful patients, guided symbolism was found to diminish agony and nervousness in patients 2 hours after surgery. It additionally can possibly upgrade understanding results and mental well-being. During a meta-investigation by Fernandez and Turk, which investigated six diverse intellectual treatments to control torment as opposed to utilizing no treatment, symbolism treatments were found to have the best impact on decreasing pain.

Guided symbolism might be utilized by all individuals from the interdisciplinary group. It has been examined by scientists including, however not constrained to, experts in the brain science, nursing, and restoration fields.

Fitting torment the executives after any medical procedure is significant in upgrading a patient's recuperation. TJR (knee or hip) is an excruciating methodology, and narcotic use in the prompt postoperative period is frequently required. Consolidating nonpharmacologic strategies may add to a general lessening in tension and enable patients to all the more likely to deal with their pain.

Uncontrolled agony following TJR frequently postpones recuperation since patients are less ready to take an interest in treatment. Inadequately oversaw agony likewise can build length of remain and abatement persistent fulfillment. Executing guided symbolism has been appeared to diminish torment and improve tolerant fulfillment scores. Therefore, more research is expected to join guided symbolism into training for patients who have experienced TJR.

Checking on the writing

Spinal and nerve squares are regularly used to diminish quick agony after elective TJR. Sentiments of torment gradually return once the anesthesia starts to wear off; uneasiness and worry about ambulating and move with the torment starts. Patients begin to figure they won't have the option to recapture practical versatility because of torment, which prompts pressure. At the point when patients are in torment, their BP and pulse may rise, causing much more pressure. Worry because of torment hinders a patient's recovery.

Guided symbolism may help reduce torment by going about as a neuromodulator, blocking torment by changing the handling in the autonomic anxious system. Nurses ought to teach patients on guided symbolism and take an interest in preparing. An integrative audit of writing led via Carpenter and partners finished up with proposals that guided symbolism be a piece of torment the executives and part of the multimodal plan of care for patients. From their exploration, the creators suggested choosing ideal recurrence and guaranteeing patients are utilizing the strategy correctly.

Torment is an emotional estimation; every patient's limit for torment is unique. The equivalent applies for the utilization of guided symbolism, as certain patients have a higher imaging capacity than others. Guided symbolism has been appeared to assist patients with speeding up, particularly in those with higher symbolism abilities. Guided symbolism and other unwinding procedures may likewise help improve rest and increment sentiments of relaxation.

Patients' impression of guided symbolism can influence results. Patients who discover the system adequate and have an uplifting viewpoint are bound to profit by the treatment. An examination investigating the agreeableness of the method by patients demonstrated that numerous patients felt it helped them unwind, diminish torment, and have a progressively positive outlook.

Nursing suggestions

Attendants are at the bleeding edge of agony the board, regulating torment drug, utilizing nonpharmacologic techniques for torment the board, for example, chilly treatment, and surveying and reevaluating a patient's clinical status. Guided symbolism ought to be remembered for preparing for overseeing postoperative consideration of patients experiencing TJR. Taking patients on a visual adventure into easing pressure and strain enables them to turn out to be progressively loose and better ready to perform exercises of day by day living. It additionally can possibly assist patients with diminishing the quantity of narcotics they take both when medical procedure. Medical caretakers must instruct patients on the addictiveness of narcotics just as illuminate them about nonpharmacologic techniques that are successful in dealing with their agony.

Lessening torment for better results

Proof recommends that guided symbolism is a powerful methodology for torment the executives of patients experiencing TJR. In any case, more examination into the point of guided symbolism ought to be directed to take into account better patient results and fulfillment in torment the board after TJR. Medical caretakers ought to comprehend the advantages of guided symbolism and the ability to actualize best practices and help patients in using it. Guided symbolism ought to be executed dependent on the patient's preference.22 Best-practice conventions and legitimate training should be completely created so as to furnish the best consideration with improved results.

Kinds of guided imagery

Unwinding symbolism includes the perception of unwinding and wonderful pictures that enable the brain and body to rest. These pictures might be new or old encounters or recollections.

Mental practice symbolism includes imagining a positive result for an uneasiness creating circumstance, for example, medical procedure or a prospective employee meet-up. The individual envisions oneself finishing each progression of the occasion, completely recouping from a medical procedure or completing the meeting with progress.

Torment control symbolism includes envisioning one's torment as something you can control by having the option to turn it off. One technique is to take one's agony and change it into something different. Another route is to envision the torment vanishing as one becomes torment free.

Utilizing guided symbolism: A model

An average guided symbolism session comprises of verbal prompts to enable the patient to unwind. Here is a model:

Close your eyes and envision yourself unwinding on a seashore someplace. Concentrate on your breath.

Journaling

A few psychotherapists are presently suggesting journaling, likewise called expressive composition, to assist individuals with adapting to the manifestations of post-horrendous pressure issues (PTSD). On the off chance that you have PTSD, here are the means by which journaling can help, just as how to do it.

Journaling is one strategy for helping individuals adapt to a horrendous accident. Expressive composing has been found to improve physical and mental wellbeing for individuals with various physical and psychological wellbeing conditions. One of the advantages of journaling is that it's economical—the expense of paper and a pen—and should be possible anyplace or whenever.

A portion of the general medical advantages of journaling incorporates improved psychological capacity, checking a large number of the negative impacts of pressure, and reinforced safe capacity.

Advantages for People With PTSD

As of late, exploration has indicated that journaling may help individuals with PTSD in a few unique manners. Mentally, expressive composing seems to assist individuals with bettering adapt to the indications of PTSD, for example, tension and outrage. Physically, journaling can have any kind of effect too, lessening body pressure and reestablishing center.

What's more, we are discovering that horrendous accidents may lead to post-awful pressure, however to post-awful development. As such, there can be silver linings and encountering injury may assist you with changing in positive manners too. Expressive composing has been found not exclusively to improve the indications of PTSD and adapting to them, yet it likewise seems to help encourage post-horrendous development, or the capacity to discover importance in and have positive life changes following an awful accident.

Diary Writing to Ease Anxiety

Before You Begin

Before journaling, discover a scratch pad and a most loved pen. A few people want to have more than one note pad, saving one to use as an appreciation diary, and the other to incorporate every other idea and emotions. You might need to consider where you will keep your diary between works. A few people like to keep it in a private area, while others don't feel this need. What's most significant is that your words are just available to the individuals who you wish to understand them.

Steps for Journaling

Follow these six stages to start journaling:

Locate a calm time and spot where there will be not many interruptions. Try not to be concerned, in any case, if there is some clamor, or on the off chance that you just have a brief timeframe. A few people find that composition at a bus stop, on a transport, or in any event, during a five-minute break during the day is useful.

Take a couple of moments to consider how your PTSD or horrendous accident has affected you and your life.

Start expounding on your most profound considerations and emotions in regards to your PTSD or the horrendous mishap you encountered. On the off chance that conceivable, compose for at any rate 20 minutes. (Note, this is perfect, however, once more, any measure of time is regularly useful, particularly on the off chance that you think that it is hard confining this measure of time each day.)

When you've got done with composing, read what you composed and focus on how you feel. Notice any adjustments in your contemplations or sentiments because of composing.

Albeit extended advantages of composting have been discovered, expounding on your PTSD or horrendous accident will normally at first raise some troubling contemplations and sentiments, so ensure you have an arrangement for how to deal with this pain.

Rehash stages 1 through 5, expounding on a similar theme for in any event two additional days. It has been discovered that expounding on a similar theme on back to back days can help arrange and improve the clearness of your contemplations and emotions about an unpleasant occasion. You might be astonished at the clearness that journaling can bring.

Journaling Tips

Here are some different tips to remember while you're composing:

Try not to stress over spelling or language structure. Concentrate essentially on getting the entirety of your musings and sentiments down.

Attempt to be as clear as conceivable in your composition. For instance, when you're depicting your sentiments, expound on the musings associated with those sentiments and how those feelings felt in your body (for example, "My heart was dashing," or "My muscles were tense."). This will help increment your mindfulness and the lucidity of your feelings and musings.

You may think that its supportive of keeping what you compose so you can see it to perceive how your considerations and emotions have changed through the span of utilizing this adapting procedure. Be that as it may, in case you're worried about others finding your compositions, you should locate a sheltered and secure method for discarding them.

It might be essential to from the outset put aside sometime each day to compose. Nonetheless, you can likewise utilize expressive composing at whatever point something unpleasant occurs. It tends to be a decent adapting system to add to your sound adapting collection.

Journaling Prompts

Here are a couple of prompts to kick you off or to proceed with when you feel stuck:

Expound on your awful experience. Be as nitty-gritty as you can with what occurred and how it affected you, both sincerely and physically.

Expound on what you gained from experience, regardless of whether it's fortunate or unfortunate.

How does the experience influence you now? Give subtleties.

What do you wish you could do any other way or change? Why?

Depict a portion of the key reasons for worry in your life now. Has this changed since your awful experience? In the event that so how? Would you be able to pinpoint why?

How did your experience sway others? This could be possibly others that were included or the individuals throughout your life now.

Is there anything you wish you had truly set aside the effort to acknowledge before the experience or that you'd offer anything to have back?

Are there manners by which you can utilize your experience to help other people? Conceptualize thoughts.

Searching for the Positive

Realizing that individuals with PTSD experience worry as well as post-horrible development may carry a little beam of light to a troublesome circumstance. A few people have discovered that setting aside the effort to expound on these constructive changes, fundamentally, expounding on appreciation, is useful as they mend.

In case you're searching for proof of post-horrible development in your life, consider anything you may call a "silver coating" of your experience. A few people talk about the "blessings of PTSD" or the "advantages of PTSD" when discussing these changes. Surely, you may need to make a stretch in doing this, particularly in the event that you have as of late created PTSD and the horrible mishap that invigorated your pain is genuinely later.

In time, and notwithstanding working through the challenges throughout your life identified with your conclusion, you may start to have minutes when you find yourself stating "what PTSD has instructed me." Expressing your musings recorded as a hard copy thusly may not just assist you with working through the dreadfulness of the injury, yet it can make you progressively mindful of your mending en route.

Hypnosis

What precisely is hypnosis? While definitions can shift, the American Psychological Association portrays hypnosis as a helpful collaboration in which the member reacts to the recommendations of the hypnotist.

Hypnosis has become understood gratitude to mainstream acts where individuals are provoked to perform surprising or absurd activities, be that as it may, it has additionally been clinically demonstrated to give restorative and helpful advantages, most eminently in the decrease of agony and tension. It has even been recommended that entrancing can diminish the side effects of dementia.

Hypnosis is maybe one of the least comprehended helpful apparatuses being used. While a great many people consider hypnosis an approach to get someone to bark like a canine at the snap of your fingers or remove their garments when you state the word 'astounding', hypnosis can be a significant instrument in helping individuals defeat fears, withstand torment, or improve their capacity to oversee worry in their lives.

In spite of prevalent thinking, it's not possible for anyone to entrance you without your assent or mindfulness. You can, be that as it may be spellbound by a prepared proficient whom you trust, to all the more effectively accomplish objectives you set for yourself. Far and away superior, you can set aside time and cash and figure out how to spellbind yourself utilizing your very own voice or even only your contemplations, a training known as self-trance.

How Does Hypnosis Work?

When you hear about a hypnosis specialist, what rings a bell? In case you're similar to numerous individuals, the word may evoke pictures of an evil stage-lowlife who realizes a hypnotic state by swinging a pocket watch to and fro.

In all actuality, hypnosis looks to some extent like these cliché portrayals. "The trance specialist doesn't spellbind the person. Or maybe, the hypnotherapist fills in as a kind of mentor or guide whose activity is to enable the individual to become hypnotized.

While hypnosis is regularly depicted as a rest like a stupor state, it is better communicated as a state described by centered consideration, uplifted suggestibility, and distinctive dreams. Individuals in a trancelike state frequently appear to be sluggish and daydreamed, yet as a general rule, they are in a condition of hyper-mindfulness.

In brain science, entrancing is at times alluded to as hypnotherapy and has been utilized for various purposes including the decrease and treatment of agony. Hypnosis is normally performed by a prepared advisor who uses perception and verbal redundancy to initiate a sleep-inducing state.

Hypnosis can be utilized for pressure the executives in two different ways. To start with, you can utilize hypnosis to get into a profoundly loosened up state, battling strain and setting off your unwinding reaction. This will forestall medical issues because of the constant pressure. Next, hypnosis can likewise assist you with accomplishing different solid way of life changes that can lessen the measure of pressure you experience in your life.

For instance, you can enter yourself to adhere to an activity program, keep your home less jumbled, feel increasingly certain defining limits with others, and so on. You can utilize hypnosis to decrease the degree of uneasiness you feel when you experience circumstances that ordinarily trigger worry too, for example, scaring social circumstances. In this equivalent vein, you can likewise viably utilize hypnosis to help conquer any negative propensities you've been utilizing to adapt to pressure, such as smoking or habitual eating.

What Effects Does Hypnosis Have?

The experience of trance can fluctuate significantly starting with one individual then onto the next. Some spellbound people report feeling a feeling of separation or outrageous unwinding during the hypnosis state while others even feel that their activities appear to happen outside of their cognizant volition. Others may remain completely mindful and ready to do discussions while under hypnosis.

Investigations by a specialist showed how trance could be utilized to significantly modify perceptions. After educating a mesmerized individual not to feel torment in their arm, the member's arm was then put in ice water. While non-entranced people needed to expel their arm from the water following a couple of moments because of the agony, the spellbound people had the option to leave their arms in the cold water for a few minutes without encountering torment.

Side effects or Conditions Hypnosis Is Commonly Used For

Coming up next are only a couple of the applications for entrancing that have been shown through research:

The treatment of constant torment conditions, for example, rheumatoid joint pain

The treatment and decrease of agony during labor

The decrease in the side effects of dementia

Hypnotherapy might be useful for specific side effects of ADHD

The decrease of sickness and regurgitating in malignant growth patients experiencing chemotherapy

Control of agony during dental techniques

Disposal or decrease of skin conditions including moles and psoriasis

Lightening of side effects related to bad-tempered inside disorder (IBS)

So for what reason may an individual choose to attempt entrancing? At times, individuals may search out hypnosis to help manage interminable agony or to lighten torment and uneasiness brought about by therapeutic methods, for example, medical procedure or labor.

Entrancing has additionally been utilized to help individuals with conduct changes, for example, stopping smoking, getting more fit, or forestalling bed-wetting.

Would you be able to Be Hypnotized?

While numerous individuals feel that they can't be mesmerized, inquire about has demonstrated that an enormous number of individuals are more hypnotizable than they accept.

Fifteen percent of individuals are extremely receptive to hypnosis.

Youngsters will, in general, be progressively defenseless to trance.

Roughly 10% of grown-ups are viewed as troublesome or difficult to spellbind.

Individuals who can turn out to be effectively invested in dreams are substantially more receptive to hypnosis.

In the event that you are keen on being mesmerized, it is critical to make sure to move toward the involvement in a receptive outlook. Research has proposed that people who see trance in a constructive light will, in general, react better.

A standout amongst other realized speculations about hypnosis is the neo-separation hypothesis of hypnosis. According to the scientist, individuals in a hypnosis state experience a split cognizance where there are two distinct floods of mental movement.

While one continuous flow reacts to the trance specialist's recommendations, another separated stream forms data outside of the entranced person's cognizant mindfulness.

Fantasies

Errors about the subject of hypnosis are normal. Here are a few legends and realities.

Fantasy 1: When you wake up from hypnosis, you won't recall that anything that happened when you were mesmerized.

While amnesia may happen in extremely uncommon cases, individuals, for the most part, remember everything that unfolded while they were mesmerized. Notwithstanding, entrancing can significantly affect memory. Posthypnotic amnesia can lead a person to overlook certain things that happened previously or during entrancing. Notwithstanding, this impact is commonly restricted and transitory.

Fantasy 2: Hypnosis can assist individuals with recollecting the careful subtleties of wrongdoing they saw.

While hypnosis can be utilized to improve memory, the impacts have been drastically overstated infamous media. Research has discovered that trance doesn't prompt critical memory improvement or precision, and hypnosis can really bring about bogus or misshaped recollections.

Legend 3: You can be entranced without wanting to.

Regardless of anecdotes about individuals being mesmerized without their assent, entrancing requires deliberate support with respect to the patient.

Legend 4: The trance inducer has unlimited oversight of your activities while you're under hypnosis.

While individuals regularly feel that their activities under hypnosis appear to happen without the impact of their will, a trance inducer can't cause you to perform activities that are against your desires.

Fantasy 5: Hypnosis can make you super-solid, quick or physically gifted.

While hypnosis can be utilized to upgrade execution, it can't make individuals more grounded or more athletic than their current physical abilities.

What's Involved

The procedure of hypnosis includes entering a daze, or a profoundly loose, yet engaged state (like that of staring off into space or contemplation), and making recommendations for your intuitive personality to acknowledge. You can go to a prepared proficient for hypnotherapy, and they will talk you through it. Or on the other hand, you can utilize the utilization of books, recordings, or even short articles to realize what's included and accomplish successful outcomes at home.

Advantages

Hypnosis is a very flexible apparatus that can be utilized for everything from straightforward unwinding to torment the board in labor. It's anything but difficult to do, can be very economical, and the outcomes are enduring. There are no potential negative symptoms, and it can give different advantages simultaneously. Once in awhile, upsetting data can come up from your intuitive personality and can be talked about and prepared in treatment. Additionally, it is essential to recollect that

Disadvantages

hypnosis is not for everybody. A few people experience difficulty moving beyond their underlying partialities about the training as a rule, and some have a progressively troublesome time getting into the stupor like state required for hypnosis recommendations to turn out to be profoundly installed. Others find that they can not discover the time or the center, and have a simpler time with different pressure the executives strategies.

How Self-Hypnosis Compares to Other Stress Reduction Methods

Like contemplation, trance requires more concentration and practice than procedures like basic exercise or the utilization of drugs and homegrown medicines, and hypnosis likewise requires some preparation or the assistance of a prepared proficient.

Notwithstanding, hypnosis might be the best choice for those with physical impediments that make practice like yoga progressively troublesome. There are scarcely any potential negative reactions, as with certain prescriptions or homegrown cures. Likewise, a couple of different systems can offer such a wide assortment of advantages. With preparing and practice, essentially anybody can utilize hypnosis somewhat of progress and experience the numerous advantages this procedure brings to the table. This is a regularly neglected yet superbly viable course to stretch help.

Exercise

When we're focused on, what's the main thing we do? Have a beverage? Provoke your life partner? Flip off the driver before you, who simply happens to be the most noticeably terrible driver on the planet? In some cases, letting out your worry in those ways can give you some brief alleviation, however, there are results, not the least of which is a furious life partner or a started driver.

At the point when you get to that point, it's difficult to think straight. In any case, the best thing you can do is most likely the keep going thing at the forefront of your thoughts—stop, take a full breath, and consider what you truly need at that time. We may float towards something that will give us moment delight (and hollering at awful drivers surely feels better, doesn't it?), however, that won't give us enduring pressure help.

What can help is accomplishing something physical, something that gets your brain and body out of that fight or flight pressure reaction and manages those pressure hormones so your body feels much improved. What's more, various types of activity can help, contingent upon how you're feeling and what you can deal with.

Basic Unstructured Activities

Regularly, as your body gets into its very own rhythms, you can release your psyche and work out issues, discover arrangements, or simply dream for a moment. Attempt these:

Work in the yard

Take a moderate bicycle ride

Go for a stroll independent from anyone else or with a companion

Wash the vehicle

Practice thoughtless or cadenced action, such as strolling, raking leaves, or wiping out drawers

Organized Exercise

Past cardio or quality preparing exercises are ideal for getting your worry leveled out. Your pulse is likely previously raised from pressure and a decent exercise will help utilize that to dispose of any additional strain and make you feel increasingly loose. A few plans to investigate include:

Interim preparing—Going hard and afterward chilling out is an incredible method to buckle down without continuing an elevated level of force for a whole exercise. Attempt these interim exercises.

High-intensity aerobics—These exercises move quick, keeping your mind drew in a while your difficulties fall away from plain sight.

Cardio works out—There's nothing superior to an old fashioned cardio exercise for making you move, consuming calories, and letting you get away from life for a brief period.

Quality preparing—Sometimes you need to feel solid in your life and, in the event that you can't feel that in your present conditions, the following best thing is feeling it in your body. Get a few loads and show the world exactly how solid you are. Attempt these quality preparing exercises.

Sex

Sex and stress are connected in a few different ways. The vast majority of us intuitively know this as of now and feel it unquestionably when an especially distressing week or two destroys us of our sex drive. Be that as it may, while stress can play a part in low drive, it can likewise be an incredible pressure reliever, which is the reason kids about anxious managers requiring a decent move in the feed are in every case useful for in any event one knowing laugh.

Have you at any point thought about what amount of truth there was to the possibility that a sound sexual coexistence works pleasantly as a pressure treatment? Here's some exploration on stress and sex.

Great Sex and Good Mood

In an Arizona State University study on 58 moderately aged ladies, physical friendship or sexual conduct with an accomplice essentially anticipated lower negative mind-set and stress, and higher positive mind-set the accompanying day.1

Basically, analysts found that sex and physical closeness drove ladies to feel less focused and be feeling better the following day. (These outcomes weren't discovered when ladies had climaxes without an accomplice.)

Positive Mood and Good Sex

A similar report found that being feeling acceptable anticipated increasingly physical friendship and sexual action with an accomplice the following day, indicating that the sex-stress the board association works the two different ways: sex can lead you to feel less pushed, and being less focused (or if nothing else feeling better) can prompt more sex. This is an additional verification of the significance of compelling pressure on the executives.

Sex and Blood Pressure

Another investigation analyzed members' circulatory strain as a proportion of their pressure reactions during open talking or testing math issues—circumstances that frequently inspire pressure. It was discovered that the individuals who had as of late engaged in sexual relations would in general have either lower gauge blood pressures, to a lesser degree a circulatory strain ascend during upsetting occasions or both.2

These discoveries recommend that having intercourse can prompt to a lesser extent a pressure reaction during testing circumstances, which is something to be thankful for.

Sex and Stress Response

Thusly, another investigation took a gander at ladies' pulse and cortisol levels as a proportion of pressure reaction and found that ladies displayed to a lesser extent a pressure reaction after 'positive physical contact' with an accomplice. Passionate help alone didn't have a similar impact.

Climax and Health

The climax itself has numerous advantages for wellbeing and stress alleviation. It can loosen up your body and discharge numerous hormones that are steady of your general wellbeing and health. This sort of unwinding can likewise be extraordinary inwardly.

Besides these logical discoveries, sex has some undeniable pressure on the executives' parts. Notwithstanding successfully removing your brain from your stresses for a tolerable timeframe, sex gives a portion of these different pressure the executives benefits:

Profound Breathing

This profound loosened up sort of breathing discharges strain and lessens the pressure you feel. The facts confirm that you can just perform breathing activities all alone and accomplish pressure the executives' benefits, however consolidating the advantages of breathing activities with the delight and closeness of sex with a caring accomplice can be so pleasant, why not do both?

Feeling of Touch

Studies show that back rub can be an extraordinary pressure reliever. Actually, we need contact for our passionate wellbeing; thinks about additionally show that infants who are not contacted enough can neglect to flourish, and contact keeps on being significant into adulthood.

The sort of unwinding, adoring touch you can trade with a decent accomplice can be an incredible pressure reliever too.

Social Support

Individuals who have a steady social outlet will, in general, oversee pressure better, live more, and appreciate expanded by and large wellbeing. The kind of enthusiastic closeness that sex can help supply is beneficial for you.

Endorphins

Sexual action discharges endorphins and other feel-great hormones. (You might be amazed by what number of, and what they do.) These synthetic substances can loosen up your body and psyche, leaving you feeling better for quite a long time a while later.

Physical Workout

Contingent upon your degree of excitement, you can consume a lot of calories during sex, and addition the pressure the executives' advantages of activity also.

Sadly, numerous individuals find that, when they're under pressure, their sex drive endures. Fortunately, with a little goal and exertion, it is conceivable to get in the state of mind in any event, when you feel unreasonably worried about sex.

Music

Music can influence the body from various perspectives, which is the reason for a developing field known as music treatment. Be that as it may, you can utilize music in your everyday life and accomplish many pressure alleviation benefits individually.

One of the incredible advantages of music as a pressure reliever is that it very well may be utilized while you direct your normal exercises so it truly doesn't remove time from your bustling calendar. Music gives a superb setting to your life and you can discover expanded happiness based on what you're doing while at the same time diminishing worry from your day.

Set up together a custom playlist for every one of these exercises and you may before long notification a critical diminishing in pressure.

When Getting Ready in the Morning

You can wake yourself up with music and start your day feeling extraordinary. By choosing the correct music, you can establish the pace for a lower-stress day.

Old style or instrumental music can assist you with awakening while at the same time keeping you quiet and centered. On the off chance that you have a major, occupied day ahead that requires additional vitality, have a go at something that is energetic and makes you need to move and grin.

During a Commute

Shut down street rage by playing your preferred music in the vehicle.

It can ease a portion of the strain you feel from the drive itself and the day up until this point.

It can assist you with feeling less like you're sitting around idly in rush hour gridlock and progressively like you're having some pleasant uninterrupted alone time.

It can remove your brain from all that you have to complete once you arrive at your goal. You will show up not so much focused but rather more arranged to take on what anticipates you.

Have a go at changing to a traditional station when you are truly worried. The relieving rhythms and sounds can quiet you down and make your drive smoother.

Cooking

Great nourishment is a significant piece of a solid way of life and it can really keep your anxiety down. Eating at home is an extraordinary method to guarantee sound suppers and more affordable, yet numerous individuals wind up too worn out to even consider cooking once they return home.

In the event that you put on some smooth jazz or a comparable type of music that you appreciate, cooking turns into an enjoyment action as opposed to a task. You will probably wind up loose and in a superior mood once supper begins, which can empower you to appreciate your supper and your organization as you eat.

While Eating

Music can likewise be a partner as you're eating your dinner. Mitigating music can trigger the unwinding reaction, which can bring down cortisol levels, making it simpler to process nourishment.

Studies have indicated that traditional music, specifically, can assist you with eating less, digest better and make the most of your nourishment more.

Cleaning

Keeping a straightforward, composed home can truly eliminate your anxiety, yet cleaning itself is a task that many occupied individuals don't have the vitality to look in the wake of a difficult day. Nonetheless, in the event that you toss on some enthusiastic music (hip-jump or fly, for instance) you can raise your vitality level and have a great time as you clean.

On the off chance that you disclose to yourself that you just need to clean for a specific measure of melodies and afterward you should be possible, you may work all the more productively. Who knows, you may even come to anticipate carrying out the responsibility.

When Paying Bills

We as a whole need to take care of tabs, yet the activity doesn't generally take a high level of fixation. Playing music while you compose your checks can help remove your brain from money related pressure you might be feeling and make the undertaking progressively agreeable.

Prior to Bed

Getting enough rest is significant for appropriate working, and getting enough rest can assist you in taking care of pressure better. Sadly, stress can likewise meddle with rest in a few different ways.

Playing music as you float off is one approach to check the impacts of worry by taking your psyche off what is focusing on you. Music can help hinder your breathing and calming your brain.

Self-Care and Stress

A huge numbers of us have such a large number of duties in life that we neglect to deal with our own needs. This is especially valid for moms, who have numerous providing care obligations, yet mothers unquestionably don't have an imposing business model on letting life impede dealing with themselves. And keeping in mind that it's difficult to organize something like scrubbing down when you have such huge numbers of different things on your plan for the day, self-care is a significant part of stress the board.

How Self Care Benefits You

We are generally less ready to deal with the anxieties that come to our direction when we're drained by physical and passionate fatigue. Or then again, put in a progressively positive way, we are stronger and increasingly ready to deal with life's pressure when we are feeling our best both physically and inwardly. A back rub, absorb the tub or different types of spoiling rejuvenate you all around. Investing significant energy to keep up self-care has a few advantages:

It Affects Your Physical Health

While self-spoiling doesn't generally prompt significant upgrades in by and large wellbeing the manner in which solid eating routine and exercise do, the unwinding you get from it can trigger the unwinding reaction, which can keep ceaseless worry from harming your wellbeing, so it might be said, self-care is beneficial for you all around.

It Affects Your Emotional Health

Investing significant energy to think about yourself can remind you and others that you and your needs are significant, as well.

Having a well-thought about the body can make you like yourself and your life, and passes on to others that you esteem yourself. This can add to extended sentiments of prosperity.

It Makes You a Better Caregiver

Individuals who disregard their very own needs and neglect to support themselves are at peril of more profound degrees of misery, low confidence, and sentiments of disdain.

Likewise, in some cases, individuals who invest their energy just dealing with others can be in danger of getting wore out on all the giving, which makes it progressively hard to think about others or themselves. Setting aside some effort to think about yourself normally can make you a superior overseer for other people.

The Importance of Self-Care

There are a few distinct approaches to concentrate on self-care, a large number of which include making time to get enough rest, organizing solid dinners, guaranteeing a parity of relaxation time in your calendar, and setting aside a few minutes for companions. A straightforward however frequently neglected type of self-care has a self-spoiling experience all the time in your very own home.

Taking a couple of hours for a spa experience and some much-merited self-care is likewise a powerful method to oversee worry for the accompanying reasons:

It Gives You a Break from Stress

Taking a break in the midst of a tub of warm air pockets or under the warm hands of an accomplished masseuse can assist you with feeling like you're getting away from an unpleasant reality and taking a psychological and enthusiastic excursion.

As recently referenced, it triggers the unwinding reaction and enables you to return to an incredible truth feeling invigorated and loose.

It Gives You Time Alone

While various individuals have changing degrees of self-preoccupation and extroversion, having some time alone is significant for the vast majority's working.

At the point when you're unwinding independent from anyone else, it's a lot simpler to slip into a condition of calm contemplation, appreciate some self-reflection, or let your issues work themselves out in the rear of your psyche, without taking the entirety of your engaged focus.

It Offers Soothing Feelings

Giving your body some uncommon treatment is a characteristic method to mitigate pressure. Other than keeping your skin delicate and your body in decent shape, spa-related exercises like a back rub and steaming showers have been known to mitigate even little colicky children like nothing else.

Such exercises keep on being viable devices for unwinding as we get more established, however we some of the time neglect to use them.

Self-Care Strategies That Work

When you've chosen it's an ideal opportunity to begin sustaining yourself and your body, make certain to close off some time for this. Attempt to plan a square where you won't be intruded. You need just to have a washroom to give yourself a home-spa experience; you can put on some calming music, and attempt a few or the entirety of the accompanying self-care methodologies.

Scrub down: Get out the air pockets, oils, and scented cleansers, and douse until you're wrinkled.

Profound Condition Your Hair: While you're in the tub, put on a profound molding treatment for your hair, and let it fill in as you unwind.

Profound Clean Your Pores: With a pleasant mud masque, you can coax contaminations out of your skin and worry about your framework.

Care For Your Feet: After you douse your feet to mellow calloused skin, utilize a pumice stone to swamp off dead skin, and finish with rich foot cream, and maybe clean.

Feed Your Skin: Rich, lavish creams smell magnificent and feel smooth, particularly on the off chance that you shed your skin in the tub before putting them on.

Watch out for Your Nails: Correct the beating your nails presumably take from your bustling life (particularly for those of you who chomp your nails!) by recording and buffing. A layer of clean can make you feel like a princess for a considerable length of time a short time later. (This is most likely more for my female perusers.)

Get a Massage: This one can be particularly decent. In the event that your financial limit doesn't take into consideration customary back rubs with an expert, check whether you can exchange with a companion or your life partner, or utilize an electronic massager.

Notwithstanding spoiling yourself, progressively significant types of self-care including the sound way of life decisions are significant, as well. Expending a solid eating regimen, getting standard exercise, and being certain you get enough rest is extremely significant for extended wellbeing and stress the executives also.

Conclusion

The polyvagal Theory gives a hypothetical Platform to decipher social conduct inside a neurophysiological context. The accentuation on phylogeny gives a sorting out rule to comprehend the various leveled succession of versatile reactions. The social commitment regulates physiological state to help positive social conduct by applying an inhibitory impact on the sympathetic sensory system. From the polyvagal theory viewpoint, social conduct is a new property of the phylogenetic improvement of the autonomic sensory system. Predictable with this progressive model, saw difficulties in endurance frequently bring about a neural disintegration from the later frameworks of positive social conduct and social correspondence to the more crude fight-to-fight and shirking frameworks. The hypothesis leads not exclusively to the clarification of the pathophysiological states related to a different clinical issue, yet additionally underpins the presentation of another worldview that may have general applications for people with diffculties in social conduct.

Printed in Great Britain
by Amazon